Front-Line
Essex

Michael Foley

SUTTON PUBLISHING

First published in the United Kingdom in 2005 by
Sutton Publishing Limited
Phoenix Mill · Thrupp · Stroud · Gloucestershire · GL5 2BU

British Library Cataloguing in Publication Data

A catalogue record for this book is available from the British Library.

ISBN 0-7509-4260-6

*To Anne, for understanding during the
many hours spent writing this book.*

Typeset in 10.5/13pt Galliard.
Typesetting and origination by
Sutton Publishing Limited.
Printed and bound in England by
J.H. Haynes & Co. Ltd, Sparkford.

Contents

Acknowledgements

The author would like to express thanks to the following for permission to use their illustrations: Essex Record Office, Ford Motor Company, Kelvedon Hatch Secret Bunker, HMSO, C. Chaloner and J. Filby. All other illustrations are from the author's private collection.

Although every attempt has been made to find the copyright owners of all the illustrations, anyone whose copyright has been unintentionally breached should contact the author through the publisher.

Introduction

Essex has always been one of the most heavily defended counties in Britain. From the earliest recorded battles in the county, when Boudicca burned the Roman town of Colchester, the men of Essex have been joined by others from all over the country when defence of the realm has been necessary. In order to stop the invasions of the Spanish, the Dutch, the French under Napoleon and the Germans in two world wars, the county became what was essentially an armed camp. This led to the building of defensive positions that have, in some cases, evolved over a period of 500 years or more to meet the changes in weaponry that have taken place. Along with the development of these fortified posts, barracks for the troops have been constructed. Before the Napoleonic period, the men lived in temporary tented camps.

Colchester, for instance, is one of the oldest garrison towns in Britain, and it has been supported by a number of less well-known establishments.

When I first became interested in the history of the military in Essex I was surprised to find that information on the many military sites in the county was quite scarce, and there were a number of sites unknown to me – perhaps because many of the books about individual barracks are either out of print or very difficult to obtain.

I have therefore done my best to include information on the main military sites that have existed in Essex and how they have evolved through the years. I hope this will provide a useful overview for those like myself who were unaware of how much influence the armed forces have had on the development of the county.

The sites, towns and military bases covered in Front-Line Essex.

ONE

The Napoleonic Years to the First World War

The end of the eighteenth century saw the beginning of the wars that followed the French Revolution and the rise to power of Napoleon Bonaparte. The wars led to a great deal of change in the military presence in Essex. For instance, until this time large summer camps had been sited around the county as gathering places for the regular army and the militia, with many of the men also being billeted in private houses and inns. Policy changed and barracks started to appear, turning many Essex towns into temporary garrisons.

CHELMSFORD

Although an ancient town with origins stretching back as far as the Roman period, Chelmsford retained its small-town appearance until the mid-nineteenth century. It was only the opening of the River Chelmer in 1797 to allow navigation from the River Blackwater and then the coming of the railway in 1843 that led to an increase in the size of the town. Chelmsford's main connection with the military was during the Napoleonic Wars, although the 32nd Foot had been stationed there in 1748.

As with other towns between London and the coast, Chelmsford was used to seeing army units marching through its streets en route for sea ports and Europe well before it had its own barracks. Of course, many of the soldiers that passed through the town were billeted on local homes or inns for short periods, and there were often complaints about the amount paid for these billets – only 5*d* a day for an infantryman; a horse was more expensive at 6*d*. There were over 8,000 soldiers billeted in Chelmsford and the surrounding area by 1794, mainly in its twenty-eight inns. To put this in context, the civilian population at this time was only just over 5,000. During the summer the troops moved to camps, such as those at Warley, but by 1795 Chelmsford had its own barracks.

Although the new barracks solved some of the problems of billeting it also raised others. For example, there was disagreement between those in control of Chelmsford and those in Moulsham over who would meet the cost of upgrading the road leading to the barracks in Moulsham. In the end Chelmsford council had to contribute to the costs. The road was built and became known as Barracks Lane.

Cartoon of Whig opposition to the war of 1797. The followers of Charles Fox and some Essex landowners held a meeting in Chelmsford during a financial crisis and mutiny in the fleet calling for the resignation of the government. The opponents of the war were shouted down by government supporters. (Essex Record Office)

Another problem was the groups of camp followers who set up home around the barracks, often in small huts.

In 1796 more barracks were built at the opposite end of the town, which helped to alleviate the overcrowding the soldiers in the first barracks had suffered. With the number of soldiers now living in the two barracks, the population of the town was again doubled.

The presence of so many soldiers caused problems, however. In 1803 there was a War Office enquiry after it was reported that soldiers were going out at night and committing robbery. The enquiry found that officers at the barracks had tried to cover up for the guilty men, and consequently, some of them were forced to leave. Eventually the only regiment left at the barracks was also forced out, leaving them empty until the outbreak of hostilities again in 1803, when they filled up once more. There was also a resumption of the practice of billeting men in inns and private houses in the town. The rates for housing a soldier had been raised since the first conflict, and many innkeepers, especially those with stables, made a good profit.

When a group of seventy Germans were billeted for one night in the stables of the Spotted Dog in Back Street in 1804, it was worth more than seventy shillings to the owner. Unfortunately the stables caught fire and thirteen men died.

The government seemed to be taking invasion threats more seriously this time and built lines of defences, including forts, that protected roads in the Chelmsford area. They stretched from the old barracks to the top of Galleywood Common and were about a mile and a half in length. One of the forts was star shaped and was armed with 48lb cannon that covered the London Road. The defences were backed up by 8,000 to 10,000 soldiers in local camps. The construction work was done by soldiers from the barracks, including members of the Lancaster Militia. Part of these defences were in the grounds of Moulsham Hall, which was owned by the Mildmay family.

As well as barracks in the town, there were camps during the summer months close by at both Danbury and Galleywood. The Galleywood area was also the site of the racecourse at Chelmsford. The course had royal patronage after George III gave 100 guineas for a race called the Queen's Shield that continued to be run until 1887. In its heyday cockfights and prize fighting contests were also held on the common.

The British victory at Waterloo in 1815 ended the war and the defences were removed, but the old barracks were not demolished until 1823. They left behind them a collection of huts still populated by camp followers in what had become a very rough area of the town.

COALHOUSE FORT

The origins of the fort in East Tilbury stretch back to one of Henry VIII's blockhouses. It was built at Coalhouse Point roughly half a mile from the fort and contained fifteen cannon. Although the armaments were increased a few years later, the blockhouse then fell into disuse. Part of the sea wall was removed and this led to flooding. The site was still derelict when the Dutch attacked the area in the seventeenth century and damaged the nearby church tower.

The wall of Coalhouse Fort facing the Thames, 2004.

The inside of Coalhouse Fort. The rails were used to carry heavy equipment.

When the French wars broke out at the end of the eighteenth century, the area was rearmed and a 24-gun battery was constructed close to the present site of Coalhouse Fort. Its battery also had barracks for the garrison. It was again disarmed after the war and it was another forty years before the battery was rearmed with more and larger guns.

The present Coalhouse Fort was part of a triangle of three new forts, two of which were in Kent at Shornemeade and Cliffe. The aim was to protect the important military establishments further up river at Purfleet and Woolwich. The forts were built when there were more problems in France in the mid-nineteenth century and another invasion scare started. A Royal Commission was set up by Lord Palmerston which recommended that nineteen new forts and over fifty batteries be built. The defences including Coalhouse were known as Palmerston Forts.

COLCHESTER

As another Essex town on the way from London to the coast, Colchester has long been used to the sight of passing soldiers. From at least the seventeenth century, many of these soldiers were billeted in inns and local homes. The beginning of the French wars led to a twenty-year spell of the army being billeted in camps on Lexden Heath and eventually in barracks in the town. By the end of the eighteenth century locals were calling for barracks to be built to stop the practice of billeting in private homes.

Colchester Castle in the early nineteenth century.

Prince Albert at Wivenhoe Park in April 1856. The Prince had come to inspect the troops at Colchester. He was shown around by Sir William O'Malley, the Barrack Master of the time.

The inspection of the East Essex Rifles, at Colchester in 1868. The building in the background is the garrison church.

The French wars and the increasing number of soldiers needed in the area because of the danger of invasion were the spur for the origin of military barracks in Colchester and several other Essex towns. In many cases these new barracks lasted only until Napoleon's defeat at Waterloo. However, in other towns, such as Colchester, barracks became a permanent fixture.

The Royal Navy was as hungry for men as the army to crew their large ships and fight the French at sea. Press gangs operated in many towns, taking unwilling hands to serve before the mast. In 1795 the government also set towns and boroughs quotas of landsmen to be supplied to the navy. These men were sought through advertisements in the local newspapers. The parish of All Saints offered 20 guineas for volunteers. Other areas had trouble in finding their quota: an advertisement offering £31 for volunteers to go to sea ran for some time in the *Chelmsford Chronicle*, but there were few takers despite the large amount of money being offered.

Colchester had not had a permanent garrison since Roman times, but that changed when barracks were built between Magdalen Street and Old Heath Road at the beginning of the nineteenth century. These were brick built, unlike the wooden huts at both Hyderabad and Meanee barracks. Cavalry barracks were also added; these could hold 3,000 men and 5,000 horses. The cavalrymen slept in a room above the stables.

The arrival of large numbers of soldiers encouraged the growth of the local market gardening industry to supply them, and this had an immediate effect on the prosperity of the area.

As well as the regular troops, who were based at the barracks, detachments of volunteers were ready to fight if the threat of invasion became a reality. These included both infantry and cavalry. The pledge these volunteers signed was worded so that their duty could include dealing with anyone who threatened the government, not just foreign enemies.

The military camp at Colchester in 1869.

War medals being presented to the troops at Colchester barracks during the Boer War.

The increased prosperity of the town during the war led to improvements that had not been possible before, such as the building of the Theatre Royal in 1812. The new building was as popular with the officers from the barracks as it was with local dignitaries. Fashionable life in the town was no doubt enriched by the presence of officers in colourful uniforms who came from the best families in the country.

After the defeat of Napoleon in 1815 most of the barracks at Colchester were shut down and sold off. However, as the *Colchester Gazette* reported in May 1816, the 1st Dragoon Guards arrived in Colchester from Hounslow and the 47th Regiment arrived at Chelmsford to lodge at the barracks.

More barracks were built in the mid-nineteenth century, and by 1855 they were big enough to house nineteen battalions. They included a field which was used as a camp by the German Legion in 1856. More huts were built that year and in 1857 married quarters were added. The German Legion returned in 1868, and many of the German soldiers married local girls while in Colchester, a tradition that was to be repeated by other foreign troops in later wars.

Throughout the nineteenth century further barracks were built in the town. Goojerat and Sabraeon were built in the early nineteenth century. The barracks had brick buildings added in 1891 to replace former wooden huts.

Also, in 1856, a garrison chapel was built, on the site of an old burial ground that had been used by previous barracks. It was named after St Alban, a citizen of Verulamium who gave his life to save a Christian priest, and could hold up to 1,500 men standing. The number was greatly reduced when seats were put in. It still serves the troops in Colchester today, and is the second largest garrison church in the country.

HARWICH

Harwich has been one of the most important Essex ports for many years, and a centre of shipbuilding and naval involvement since the earliest military events in British history. The majority of the soldiers who travelled through Essex towns on their way to Europe headed there.

Daniel Defoe, on his tour of England in 1774, said of Harwich that the harbour was covered by a strong battery of guns. The guns he meant were probably on the Suffolk side of the river in Landguard Fort, but it was built so far out into the river that it was at that time seen to be in Essex. In 1667 one of the largest armed landings by an enemy force since 1066 took place at Landguard when the Dutch invaded but were beaten off.

Once again it was the war against Napoleon that spurred the need to fortify the port of Harwich on the Essex side of the river, although troops had been billeted there before this. The East Essex were at Harwich in 1782 and the Hertford Militia camped there in 1796. There is no doubt that the Harwich military camp was as big as the other summer military camps in Essex.

Harwich in the mid-nineteenth century with the defences on the left.

Landguard Fort and the entrance to Harwich Harbour, 1888. The fort was originally seen as being in Essex, although it was on the Suffolk side of the river.

One of the early iron-clad warships, HMS Essex.

The cruiser Blenheim *(left) ran aground at Harwich in 1909.*

Beacon Field was the site of the first Harwich barracks in 1795, and these were followed two years later by more on Barrack Field. Harwich was the headquarters of the eastern district of the Engineers. In addition to the 2,000 regular soldiers and 120 horses in the new barracks, a force of local volunteer infantry was also enlisted. The Loyal Harwich Volunteers had the mayor, John Hopkins, as their first captain and were trained by militiamen.

Admiral Nelson came to Harwich during the French Wars to help organise a volunteer force of Sea Fencibles in the area, but he never came ashore from his ship *Medusa*. The Sea Fencibles were a reservist force for the navy and numbered nearly 500 men. They were immune from the press gangs that roamed the area, looking for recruits. The Fencibles also manned floating batteries. These had been anchored in the entrances to the rivers Blackwater, Colne and Orwell.

In 1808 a redoubt was built overlooking the mouth of the River Stour to stop a French naval force sailing into the port. The building of the redoubt meant that the road to Dovercourt had to be rerouted to its present location. The redoubt is thought to have been built mainly by French prisoners of war.

The Harwich Redoubt was one of three built in the south; the others were at Dymchurch in Kent and Eastbourne in Sussex. The redoubts were part of a coastal defence system that stretched round the south coast and up into Essex and Suffolk. The defences consisted mainly of a line of Martello towers along parts of the coast. By then it was a common belief that the most likely landing place in Essex for an invasion force would be at Clacton, which was the reason for the Essex Towers being mainly positioned along the beach there and at nearby Walton on the Naze.

Although part of the same defence system as the Martello towers the redoubt at Harwich was of a completely different construction. It was 200ft in diameter, had a moat and could house 300 troops. It was armed with ten 24lb cannon. The fort was built on a hill on the site of Hill House, which was demolished to make way for it. It took three years to build the defences.

Following the construction of the redoubt, a further defence was erected in 1811. This was the Bathside Battery, which was built to protect the west side of the town. It was much smaller than the redoubt and had only three 24lb cannon.

There was a large garrison at Harwich throughout the Napoleonic Wars, both as a barrier to an invasion and to guard the shipyards. A number of large warships of up to seventy-four guns were built in the local dockyards. After the war these were scaled down and most were demolished a few years later.

MALDON

This is one of the best-known historical areas of Essex, mainly owing to the battle with an invading Viking army that took place there. Maldon had an important role in the county after this. It was a busy port by the fourteenth century, at a time when the poor roads made river transport much more reliable than land. Although there were plans to connect Maldon with Chelmsford by canal, it was eventually decided that the canal would go to Heybridge instead, which was a serious blow to business in Maldon.

In keeping with its military past there were barracks at Maldon. They were built at the end of the eighteenth century and lasted until after Napoleon's defeat. Between 1807 and 1833 barracks also existed in London Road. Many of the new houses of the period in Maldon were built by officers from the barracks, who preferred to live in the luxury to which they were accustomed rather than in the basic conditions at the barracks.

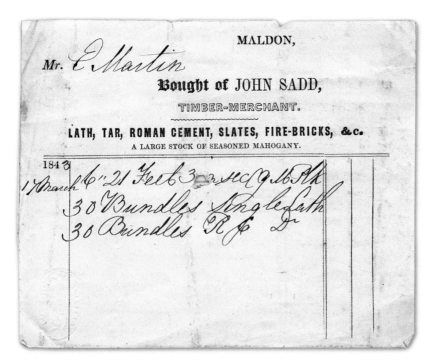

Receipt from John Sadd from 1843. The company supplied much of the material for the wooden huts in the barracks that were built in Essex during the early twentieth century.

A church parade for the Essex Regiment at Maldon.

The siting of the barracks at Maldon was no doubt partly due to the danger of an invader using the rivers close by. The view was that the Colne was probably too difficult for an invading force to navigate; the Crouch could only be navigated by soundings; and the Blackwater only by local fishermen.

However, a report on Essex defences written in 1805 pointed out that if an invading force did manage to navigate the Blackwater, then several places were suitable for landing troops. This was especially true of parts of the north bank, which were accessible for two to three hours at high tide.

Not much seems to be known about the Maldon barracks but there are a number of soldiers from the period buried in the local churchyard. Although some of these deaths may have been due to wounds received in war, they could also have been caused by the poor conditions that soldiers lived in at this time.

The barracks were shut once peace was restored and were put up for sale in 1816. The land and fixtures were advertised in the *Star* newspaper in August 1816. They were to be auctioned to the public by a Mr R.H. Kelham under the authority of the Commissioner for the Affairs of Barracks.

PURFLEET

Purfleet's most important connection with the military was the gunpowder magazine, which was built next to the Royal Hotel on the bank of the Thames. It was not the only magazine built by the river or in Essex. The first in the county was built in the mid-sixteenth century in Waltham Abbey. Barges full of gunpowder travelled down the River Lea to the Thames and on to Woolwich and Purfleet.

There were five magazine buildings about 50yds from the bank of the Thames, each holding over 10,000 barrels of powder. The buildings could withstand explosions and the men working in them were supplied with special safety equipment and uniforms. The magazine area of about 25 acres had a protective wall around it. There was also a large house on the hill above the magazine for the storekeeper.

The danger of magazines became even more obvious when nine people and four horses were killed in an explosion at the Waltham Abbey mills at the

The exterior of one of the five powder magazines, 1868. (Essex Record Office)

Loading a powder barge at Purfleet Quay, 1868. The powder arrived and left the magazine by river. (Essex Record Office)

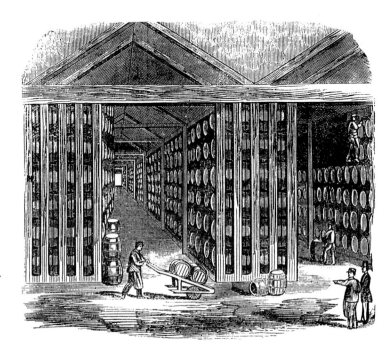

The interior of one of the powder magazines showing how the barrels were stored, 1868. (Essex Record Office)

beginning of the nineteenth century. This led the Committee of Royal Security to visit Purfleet to examine the dangers of the site.

The presence of troops in the area caused another problem: in 1813 the church at nearby Aveley had to build a gallery so that the locals and members of the Royal Artillery from Purfleet could all fit into the building.

In 1836 the Purfleet coastline of chalk cliffs and large caverns, which is peculiar to this part of the Thames, was described as romantic. There was a harbour at the river's mouth and the Beacon Cliffs overlooked the village. A large number of the local inhabitants worked in the chalk and lime pits owned by local businessman William Whitbread.

Rifle ranges were added to the site later and were well used. In 1866 the 1st Middlesex Artillery held their annual carbine shooting prize meeting at Purfleet. There were prizes ranging from £3 to £10. First prize was won by a Corporal Meens. There were also consolation prizes for women.

For a short period in the early nineteenth century, gunpowder was also kept in floating magazines anchored on the Thames at Galleon's Reach, and there were two

Purfleet was graced by the presence of many different regiments during its lifetime. In 1889 a detachment of the 2nd Battalion the Buffs, the Royal East Kent Regiment, were at the barracks. They are seen here in a carefully posed photograph with some men astride cannon.

Although the Buffs only had to cross the Thames to reach Purfleet, I doubt that they did it on this fine raft that they have built.

others anchored near Purfleet Creek. The *Conquistador* and the *Mermaid* were used from the end of the Crimean War until 1868–70 because the magazine was full.

There was a strict curfew at the magazine, and everyone had to be inside the walls by nine and have all lights and fires extinguished by ten thirty. Not all the workers at the magazine were members of the armed forces.

It seems strange now but security at the magazine was not a high priority in its early days. For instance, at the end of the nineteenth century the fire engine house in the magazine was used for a public market, and one of the landlords of the Royal Hotel used to put on plays in the camp which were attended by the locals.

By the late nineteenth century, however, security was being tightened. Between 1870 and 1873 new concrete huts were added for extra troops; the garrison then had up to eighty artillerymen stationed there. Extra troops were also brought in during 1878 when there were rumours of a suspected Fenian attack on the site. The police were also involved, and all civilian staff were enlisted to help guard the magazines.

Purfleet in the mid-nineteenth century. The magazine is just visible on the bank of the river.

ROMFORD CAVALRY BARRACKS

The majority of the barracks opened by the new Barrack Department in the late eighteenth century were for cavalry. Romford was one of a string of camps placed at strategic points around the county. The barracks built there in 1795 was one of the larger ones, big enough for six troops of cavalry. They were built to counter the threat of invasion by Napoleon's forces, and still in existence long after Napoleon had been incarcerated on St Helena.

The camp was built on 12 acres of land situated between what is now Waterloo Road, previously Dog Lane, and High Street. It was very close to the Workhouse, which was just outside the main town. The Prince of Wales, the future George IV, reviewed the troops at the barracks not long after they opened. This inspired a patriotic response from the local people, it being said that all local men were willing to take up arms and fight the French.

When the inspection took place, also present were the Havering Company of volunteer cavalry, of which there were three troops of volunteers by 1802, numbering 120 men. These were part of a wider group of volunteer cavalry throughout the country, rather like the Home Guard of the Second World War, and seemed to have had the same shortages of weapons as their later counterparts – when one squad were given swords, they had to return their pistols.

The 7th Earl of Cardigan (1797–1868) is remembered throughout the world as a great hero, although he achieved this fame much later than the Napoleonic period. Poems were written about his greatest military success and films made about the Charge of the Light Brigade he led in 1854. What is not as well known is that at the beginning of his military career he was posted to Romford.

The Earl of Cardigan was not the only member of the aristocracy stationed in Romford. Lord George Bentinck was the second son of the 4th Duke of Portland, and while in Romford he lived in a large double-fronted building in High Street known as Queen's House. It was called this because Princess Charlotte had stayed there in 1761 when on her way to marry George III.

The only traces the area now has of the barracks is the name Waterloo Road and a gravestone in St Edward's churchyard belonging to James Ryder Mowatt, master of the barracks during the Napoleonic Wars and up until his death in 1823. Mowatt was a captain in the 28th Regiment of Infantry.

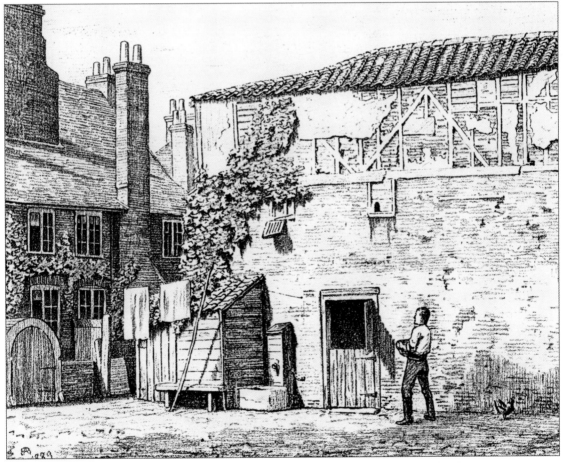

The remains of Romford Barracks a few years after its closure. (Essex Record Office)

The gravestone of James Ryder Mowatt, Master of Romford Barracks. The gravestone is in the churchyard of St Edward's Church, Romford Marketplace, but is no longer on the site of the grave. It is thought that the grave is underneath an extension to the church hall.

SHOEBURYNESS

Shoeburyness had a very early experience of military inhabitants when it became the site of a Viking camp in the ninth century. In fact two Danish armies camped there at one time before beginning separate pillaging expeditions.

The artillery-testing range at Shoeburyness had a similar beginning to that of the gunpowder magazine at Purfleet. The original artillery-testing site had been at Woolwich like the magazine, but the missiles fired there often went out into the Thames, posing a threat to passing boats. As traffic on the river increased, it became too dangerous, and a new more remote site was looked for. Once again it was the marshes of the Essex coastline that were chosen for dangerous military uses.

The site at Shoeburyness had originally been a signal station during the Napoleonic Wars. The six old coastguard cottages and buildings at Rampart House Farm were taken over in 1847–8. Barracks were built in 1852. The area was still very remote when the artillery site was opened, and the local population small. Many of the first officers at the site stayed at the Royal Hotel in Southend.

At first the site was used only in the summer and abandoned during the winter, following the lead of the old military camps of Essex. All types of artillery were tested, including shells and rockets. Some of the bigger guns caused problems for locals when they were fired. On occasions houses in the village were damaged by the shock of the explosions, and despite shelters being built, there were also a number of injuries and some deaths caused by guns and ammunition exploding.

Experiments with the Armstrong 600-pounder against the Warrior *floating target off Shoeburyness in 1863.*

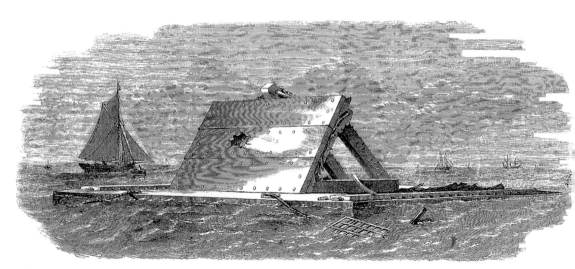

The target from the front.

The target from the rear.

The National Artillery Association shooting for the Queen's Cup at Shoeburyness in 1867.

Although there was extensive testing of many weapons at Shoeburyness, when the Crimean War came, which was the first conflict that Britain had experienced for forty years, it was found that many of the army's weapons were out of date. Because of this Shoeburyness finally became a permanent testing site.

There was a very relaxed attitude to security in the early years of the camp. Sightseers often came up from Southend to watch the experiments. The nearby coastal resort had recently become an attraction for visitors and no doubt the testing station added to the excitement of a visit. At times civilians were only yards away from the guns as they fired. There was even a case of two young boys being killed while trying to carry off an unexploded shell.

There was a report on the condition of the barracks in 1867 which described them as very good. There was a hospital which was flanked on both sides by cottages for non-commissioned officers. The cottages had flower gardens at the front and kitchen gardens at the rear. Across the parade ground from the hospital were some wooden huts for soldiers, but the main living quarters were the brick-built buildings around the perimeter wall of the camp.

In 1874 Prince Louis Napoleon spent some time at Shoeburyness. He later went on to die in Africa fighting for England in the Zulu Wars. In the same year soldiers from the barracks were sent to help the police in Southend when there were two

Amateur theatricals were a popular pastime in the Victorian army. Shoeburyness had a very active theatre group for many years. This is a rare photograph of a production in 1870.

The title Rose Bud of Stinging Nettle Farm *and the exaggerated poses of the cast show that productions of the 1870s were highly melodramatic.*

Experiments at Shoeburyness on the Plymouth Breakwater Target, 1868. Note the splinter-proof shelter for spectators.

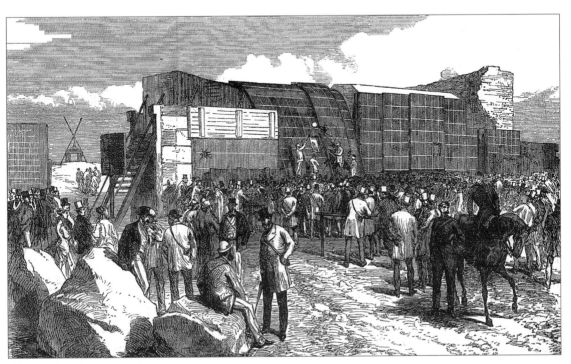

Examining the target after firing.

While the artillery was busy at Shoeburyness, the Navy was showing its might at a Naval Review at Southend.

days of running battles there between rival gangs from the East End of London. The bank holiday battles between Mods and Rockers at seaside resorts in the 1960s were nothing new.

Accidents continued to happen, and in 1885 a shell exploded while being loaded into a gun. The explosion killed several men including officers. The popularity of the soldiers within the local community was made clear when the whole of Southend and Shoeburyness shut down as a mark of respect during the funerals.

TILBURY FORT

The first fortifications at Tilbury resulted from Henry VIII's review of coastal defences. As he spent much of his reign offending fellow monarchs in Europe, this was something he felt he could not ignore. He had blockhouses built in East and West Tilbury in 1540. The western blockhouse was later to become part of Tilbury Fort. Although the defences did not see any action, the site was still seen as strategic in the defence of the capital.

In 1588 a camp for troops was created close to the fort in response to the threat of the Spanish Armada. Queen Elizabeth visited the camp wearing armour and gave her famous rousing speech, saying although she had the body of a weak and feeble woman, she had the heart and stomach of a king.

The fort fell into disrepair and remained so until the Dutch attacks in the Thames in the seventeenth century. Work on strengthening Tilbury began soon after. The fort stood alone on the banks of the Thames in the unhealthy Essex marshes, and by the time of the outbreak of the French Wars at the end of the eighteenth century its remote position made Tilbury an unpopular posting. Recruits billeted at the fort were locked in at night to stop desertion, and the officers spent as much time as possible across the river at the more fashionable Gravesend.

In 1780 5,000 troops crossed the river from Dartford and set up camp behind the fort. They carried out a mock attack to test its defences. In 1797, during the naval mutiny at the Nore, the 49th Regiment of Foot was sent to Tilbury along with the Warwickshire Militia. Their task was to stop the mutineers reaching the ships moored at Long Reach.

During the early eighteenth century barracks were added to the fort as part of the attempt to turn Essex into a large armed camp to combat the danger of invasion. The barracks were manned by recruits, who were often quickly moved on to fight in Europe. As a means of joining the forts on opposite sides of the Thames, tunnels to

The elaborate gateway of Tilbury Fort in the early nineteenth century.

Landing heavy guns at Tilbury Fort, 1871. Note the large size of the gate in the drawing.

link Tilbury and Gravesend were planned. A shaft was sunk in 1803, but the tunnel was never completed. A number of armed hulks were moored across the river between Tilbury and Gravesend to reinforce the firepower of the forts.

Tilbury was mainly only a transit camp but the conditions in the Essex marshes nevertheless made it a very unhealthy place for troops. There was a great danger of fever in this and other areas along the banks of the Thames.

Once the French Wars were over the garrison of the fort became a mixed bag of men from various regiments, including some artillerymen who were invalids. During this period Lieutenant-Colonel John Midgley was commandant at the camp from 1815 to 1826.

During the Crimean War, the army's experience of fighting against coastal forts showed those in command how valuable they could be. It was therefore decided to move London's first line of defence closer to the sea. Tilbury then became part of the second defensive line, and this is probably the main reason that it has survived in its present condition and has not been brought up to date.

In 1868 General Gordon, who later became famous for his fatal defence of Khartoum in 1885, took control of the fort. Gordon had come to live in Gravesend in 1865 at the age of 32, and he was already known as Chinese Gordon after putting an end to the civil war in China. He became Commandant of the Thames Forts with the duty of reconstructing and updating them.

WARLEY

The origins of military involvement at Warley go back well into the eighteenth century, if not earlier, when Brentwood was the mustering point for large numbers of militia from all over Essex for many years. Camps were set up on Warley Common where the militia would spend some of the summer months training while living in tents.

The American War of 1776, closely followed by the French Wars, led to a more organised situation in which the militia was called out to reinforce the army. The threat of a possible invasion by the French led to the stationing of a large armed force in Essex, and when a huge French army was assembled in Brittany in preparation for invasion, Warley was chosen as the site where the militia could train with the regular army and be close to any point where the French might land. Both groups shared the same camp. In addition, men came from all over the country to swell the numbers and help prepare a force to meet the invasion threat.

The camp on Warley Common was well known, because the area had also been used for horse race meetings. As well as followers of the sport of kings, other people began to visit the area to watch the troops. The camp became a tourist hot spot, and this led to the opening of several inns. At first they were related to the racing, such as the Horse and Jockey and the Turf Tavern, but later alehouses took on more military-sounding names, such as the Soldier's Hope.

The camps became quite large, considering that they were still only temporary, and by 1778 there were over 7,000 troops stationed there. These included three regular regiments and eleven of militia. Warley received some celebrity visitors as well as normal tourists. In 1778 Samuel Johnson visited the camp and spent a week

Both sides of the Warley halfpenny. The coin was produced to commemorate the visit to the camp by the Prince of Wales in 1794. It has an inscription on the edge that reads 'Warley Camp Halfpenny'.

THE WARLEY HEROES OR THE LIGHT INFANTRY ON FULL MARCH.

Late eighteenth-century print, The Warley Heroes.

there, staying in a tent with a friend who was an officer in the militia, and two even greater celebrities, George III and Queen Charlotte, visited later the same year. By then the camp held 10,000 men. The royal couple were treated to the sight of a large mock battle. No doubt they also had a musical accompaniment, as the camp had acquired a band by this time.

Despite being a part-time camp Warley was still run on strict military lines, at least for the enlisted men. A number of deserters were caught in 1779 and were sentenced to 1,000 lashes each. Only about half of the punishment was carried out before the victims were taken off to hospital. The whole sentence could have been fatal.

In the days before barracks were built in England wives, girlfriends and prostitutes would trail behind their men from place to place, even following them into war. This was no doubt true of Warley.

Even when the first barracks were built conditions in them were not good. Large numbers of men shared rooms; often several men shared a bed. The few men who did receive permission to bring wives into the barracks, usually six men per company, had to make do with a blanket as a screen between them and the other occupants of the room as their only means of privacy. This was known as the corner system and was criticised as indecent. Despite this the development of married quarters was a long way off.

THE ESSEX REGIMENT

Badge of 1st Battn.   Old Shako Plate,
2nd Battn., 1811

Main picture: *The Essex Regiment at the Battle of Drienfontein during the Boer War in 1900.*
Inset: *The Essex Regiment badge.*

A few years later something was to happen a long way from Warley that would have a lasting effect on the barracks at a later date. The 44th Regiment of Foot was serving in Canada in 1782 when they received a letter stating that from that date they would be called the East Essex Regiment. The theory behind the move was that connecting infantry regiments to parts of the country would encourage local men to join them. Later, in 1881, the 44th became the first battalion of the Essex Regiment. The second battalion was the 56th Regiment, the third battalion the Essex Rifles and the West Essex Militia became the fourth battalion. The Essex Regiment was later to have long-lasting connections with Warley.

Along with other camps in Essex, the occupants of Warley were sometimes called on to deal with domestic as well as international strife. In July 1795 a riot broke out because of high food prices at Saffron Walden. Lord Cornwallis, the commander of Warley at the time, had to refuse to send men to deal with the riot as he only had untrained members of Pembrokeshire Fencibles at the camp. The Surrey Light Dragoons from Lexden Camp were sent instead.

During the postwar period the East India Company was expanding its operations across the world. In 1843 the Company purchased Warley Barracks for £15,000, mainly because the camp had a hospital and was bigger than their old barracks site. During this period the men from Warley were regularly sent to India.

After the Indian Mutiny the government took over the administration of India and began to send regular troops to the country, so there was no longer any need for the East India Company to have their own forces. In 1860 the government therefore bought Warley back from the company.

WEELEY BARRACKS

In 1803, when invasion fears were at their strongest, barracks were built in Weeley, which was a small village at the time. When the military left after the French Wars, the population was still under 1,000.

Several batteries were built in the late eighteenth century along the Clacton coast. However, it was realised that these alone would not be enough of a deterrent to an invading force unless backed by a large number of troops. That was the main reason for Weeley's construction.

It was quite a large barracks, consisting of wooden huts built on brick plinths, and it contained a hospital and a rifle range. This latter was an important part of the barracks, as any recruit who had never fired a gun had to make at least fifteen shots. The builder was Alexander Copeland, who also built barracks in Chelmsford. He was awarded the contract in July 1803 and the barracks were to be completed by September the same year. The barracks were meant to hold over 4,000 men and over 200 horses.

Weeley was mainly used to house Scottish regiments. The Gordon Highlanders were marched from Glasgow to Leith and embarked for Weeley at the outbreak of hostilities in 1803, their destination being described as the new camp being set up at Weeley. A second battalion, numbering 1,000, was enlisted in Scotland, and this was to be a nursery for the regiment. They also returned to Weeley later in the war.

Account of Hay, &c, delivered at Weeley Barracks 1807, to the
Accot of G. H. Munnings &Co, at 3.17.6 ⅌ ton, including the
charge of 3.6 ⅌ ton for trussing ——

1807			£ s d
Jan 17. deliver'd at Weeley,	2 Tons of Hay		7. 15. 0
19. Do	2 Do		7. 15. 0
20. Do	2 Do		7. 15. 0
Do	1½ Do of Shaw		3. 0. 0
21. Do ⅌ Mayhew	2 Tons of Hay		7. 15. 0
Do ⅌ Farmer	2 Do		7. 15. 0
22. Do	2 Do		7. 15. 0
Do	1½ Do of Shaw		3. 0. 0
24. Do ⅌ Farmer	2 Tons of Hay		7. 15. 0
Do ⅌ Mayhew	2 Do		7. 15. 0
27. Do ⅌ Farmer	2 Do		7. 15. 0
Do ⅌ Osborne	1½ Do of Shaw		3. 0. 0
29. Do ⅌ Farmer	2 Tons of Hay		7. 15. 0
31. Do	2 Do		7. 15. 0
Feby 12. Do	2 Do		8. 0. 0
13. Do	2 Do		8. ~ ~
14. Do	2 Do		8. ~ ~
16. Do	2 Do		8. ~ ~
19. Do	2¼ Do		9. ~ ~
21. Do	2¼ Do		9. ~ ~

£ 144. 5. 0

½ £ = 72. 2. 6

April 9th ½ of the above is entered in the Priory Accot
& the other ½ in the Farming Accot

A receipt for the purchase of hay for Weeley barracks in 1807. (Essex Record Office)

One of the surviving Martello towers at Clacton. This one is at Tower Avenue close to the pier and was adapted for use by the coastguard.

The tower by Clacton Golf Course. The Hastings Avenue tower is just visible to the right of the block of flats in the distance. The four towers at Clacton must have been within sight of each other before modern buildings interrupted the view.

Another redundant Clacton tower at Hastings Avenue car park.

A Martello tower on the Martello caravan site, Walton on the Naze.

The Black Watch also embarked from Leith in 1803 on their way to the new barracks. They only numbered 400 as 475 men had been discharged the previous year due to the short-lived peace. A second battalion of 1,343 men was later raised in Scotland and embarked from Fort George to join the first battalion at Weeley. In October of that year they left Weeley and marched to Plymouth for Gibraltar. Weeley later became the centre of defence of north-east Essex.

The troops quickly became part of local life, sometimes with tragic consequences. In nearby Little Clacton there were regular fairs, and in 1806 many of the soldiers from Weeley visited one. This led to a near riot between the soldiers and local civilians. There was further trouble later at the Blacksmith's Arms. After being soundly beaten by the soldiers, a number of the locals lay in wait for them as they returned to the barracks. They were attacked and one soldier was murdered with a grindstone handle. His name was Alexander McDonald of the 1st Battalion 79th Regiment, and he is buried in Weeley churchyard. During the First World War his headstone was restored by members of the Queen's Own Cameron Highlanders who were stationed in the area.

A number of Martello towers were built in the Clacton area in 1809, as it was seen as one of the most likely invasion sites in Essex. It seems a strange time for this work, as Napoleon's navy had been severely damaged at the Battle of Trafalgar and the danger of invasion had receded. The total cost of the towers was reported as £225,000, a colossal amount for that time for defences that were never used.

Because much of the Essex coast was so unhealthy, because of the marshes that lined it, the garrisons of the Martello towers were not forced to live in them. The plan was to man them only when needed. As all the towers in the Clacton area were within a few hours marching time of Weeley Barracks, the tower garrisons were based there.

If the location of the Martello towers was unhealthy, that of the barracks at Weeley was not much better. The mortality rate for civilian men between 20 and 40 years of age was 9.8 per 1,000 in the middle of the nineteenth century. In the barracks among what would have been expected to be fit young men, it was 17.1. No doubt the figures would have been worse earlier in the century.

Archibald Foulkes wrote scathingly that when a man joined the army it was for life, or until his bodily vigour was so impaired that he was no longer fit for service. What with cholera in India and yellow fever in the West Indies, poor fare in barracks and noxious crowded transports, no great number of soldiers stayed alive long enough to get a pension.

Weeley does not seem to have been much healthier than the Martello towers on the coast. There was an outbreak of typhus in the camp and over 700 men caught it, but none died. By July many of its inhabitants left again for Walcheren in the Netherlands, a disastrous campaign due to the sickness and fever that struck the whole expeditionary force, including the Cameron Highlanders.

One of the windows in the church at Dovercourt was presented by the German Kaiser in memory of the German soldiers who perished alongside our own in the doomed Walcheren expedition. The window was put in the church at Dovercourt because many of the sick troops returned from the ill-fated expedition to nearby Harwich.

TWO

The First World War to the Second World War

With the outbreak of the First World War Essex once again began to fill up with troops. At first these men were trained and sent out to the battlefields of France that were scenes of enormous slaughter. The danger of invasion then led to a more defensive use of the men. This war was different from any of those that came before. German airships and planes brought the war to the residents of the county, by bombing civilian targets, which no one in the country had ever experienced before.

The Essex Regiment at North Weald, 1907. There seem to have been military camps in many parts of Essex at various times.

A military camp somewhere in Essex before the First World War.

The Zeppelin crews who bombed England were given a very bad press by the British media. A favourite form of abuse was to call the crews 'baby killers'. The Germans responded with propaganda postcards, such as this one showing the crew of a crashed Zeppelin that a British fishing boat supposedly left to drown.

Troops being reviewed at Rayleigh in the First World War period.

CHELMSFORD

The military presence in Chelmsford had finally ended when the local militia were moved to Warley in 1880. However, a drill hall built for the Chelmsford Volunteers had been opened by Field Marshal Lord Roberts and Field Marshal Sir Evelyn Wood in 1903. There were also a number of military parades in the town by reservists in the years before the war.

Chelmsford had still not lost its small town atmosphere by the beginning of the First World War, but they were involved in it at once. The Essex Yeomanry gathered in the town on the morning of the outbreak of hostilities and set off for the railway station to begin their journey to France. In the next four years they were followed by thousands more local men.

Within months of the outbreak of the war King George V visited the town and inspected the South Midland Division, a territorial unit, who were paraded at Hyland's Park.

When men enlisted in the army in the Chelmsford area they were often put up at a pub for the first night before being marched to Chelmsford the next day. The tradition of billeting men in pubs and private houses was still alive and well. Sometimes the men ended up in regiments other than the one they thought they had joined.

Chelmsford High Street, pre-First World War, showing Boer War cannon.

The Corn Exchange, Chelmsford, was converted into Soldiers' Hall during the war.

As with other barracks built during the First World War many of the men lived in large huts. Most of the huts used in Essex barracks during the war came from a carpentry company based in Maldon. Sadds Carpentry dated back to 1729, when it had moved from Chelmsford to Maldon. They made hutments, doors and window frames to supply the numerous barracks that sprang up in the county during the conflict. The huts were then usually erected by the soldiers themselves.

There were efforts to provide amusements for the men who flooded into the town to answer the call to defend their country. The Empire Cinema was built during the war years.

Through the manufacturers in the area, Chelmsford did much to supply munitions and armaments during the First World War. Camps were established for the many soldiers stationed in the area, and in many cases, such as in the camp in Broomfield, the men lived in tents, as they had in the Essex military camps of the eighteenth and nineteenth centuries.

Many soldiers were again also billeted in private homes and public houses, and in any building that could be used for housing troops. The old campsite on Galleywood Common was again used by an artillery regiment, who actually lived in the racecourse stand. In 1917 the building was damaged by the soldiers using it, for which the racecourse later obtained £230 in compensation from the army.

In the town itself several buildings were given over to military use. For example, the Corn Exchange became a recreation hall for soldiers and the museum a military hospital, with wooden huts erected in the grounds for use as extra wards.

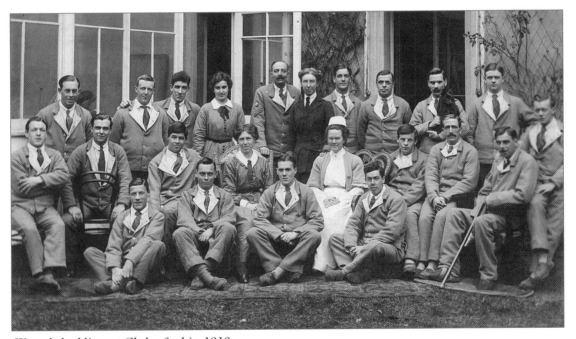

Wounded soldiers at Chelmsford in 1918.

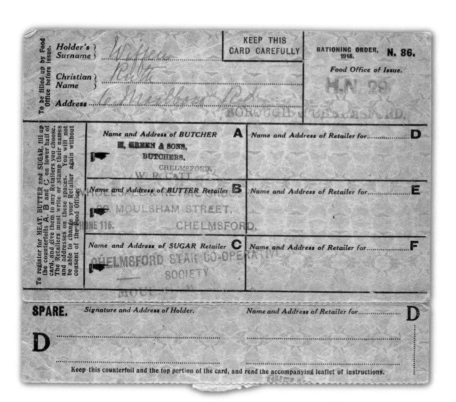

*First World War
ration card for
Chelmsford, showing
the names of retailers.*

The end of the war brought changes to Chelmsford, as it did to the rest of the county. Taxes were high and there was a shortage of workers owing to the number of men killed in France. It was difficult for the local gentry to find enough servants to run large estates. This was one of the reasons that many of these estates were sold and the land often used for building more humble housing. This led to a great change in the local area, including the influx of more industry, which now had a workforce from the people living in the new housing.

COALHOUSE FORT

By the First World War Coalhouse Fort had become almost obsolete as a defensive position due to the improvement of weapons and the stronger defences that had been erected nearer the coast. However, the fort was still used as a defensive station on the river route to London and against air attacks. The Royal Garrison Artillery was sent there to man the guns. Searchlights were fitted and operated by the London Electrical Engineers. A minefield was set up in the river and an old warship, the *Champion*, was moored in the river by the fort. Boats from the warship checked any incoming vessel while the guns in the fort covered them.

The fort became a training camp for soldiers who would then be shipped out to fight in the trenches in France. As well as using barracks inside the fort itself, the men followed old traditions and lived nearby in tents and in local houses.

The exterior of Coalhouse Fort, showing the businesslike appearance of the building, 2004.

A plaque in the church tower thought to have been damaged by the Dutch attack in the seventeenth century and partly rebuilt by First World War soldiers from the fort. The plaque near Coalhouse Fort commemorates the First World War and General Gordon.

Anti-aircraft guns were set up close to the fort and were often in use against Zeppelins and aircraft on their way to bomb London. The only real action against a foreign enemy that the fort was involved in was in firing on Zeppelins as they attacked the south-east. The gunners at the fort were successful in destroying at least one of the airships.

Some of the soldiers stationed in the fort had the idea of rebuilding the tower of St Katherine's Church, which had been destroyed by the Dutch attack in the seventeenth century. Although they received permission to do this, it seems that no one informed the commanding officer, and they were unfortunately ordered to stop before they completed the task. There is, however, a large stone plaque (see p. 49) in the outside wall of the tower commemorating those from the fort who died in the First World War and General Gordon of Khartoum, who once commanded the forts on the Thames.

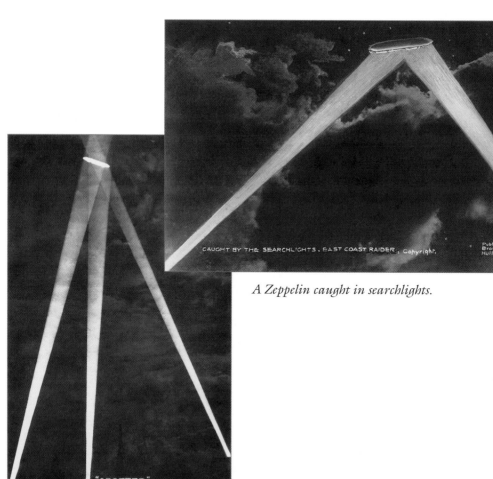

A Zeppelin caught in searchlights.

Coalhouse Fort was equipped with searchlights in the First World War to spot the Zeppelins flying over on the way to bomb London.

COLCHESTER

The infantry barracks in Colchester were rebuilt in 1898, but despite the new brick buildings many of the wooden huts built in the mid-nineteenth century were still in use in 1900. The real change came a few years later with the outbreak of the First World War. More huts were built to house the thousands of recruits, on their way to the trenches in France, who swamped the town. Most of these were volunteers, but there were also reservists, and they all arrived in civilian clothes and needed to be fitted out with uniforms and equipment. Many of these men never returned; others did, but often seriously wounded.

One of the major events of the First World War occurred in 1916 when Zeppelin L33 was hit by gunfire while trying to reach London on a bombing raid. It was forced to land close to the village of Little Wigborough. The crew of twenty-two did not fit the description that propaganda had given the population. Far from being baby killers, they warned the villagers of the danger before setting fire to the airship. Carrying one of the crew who was wounded, they set off towards Colchester and surrendered to a policeman who found them walking along the road.

Although rationing did not occur until late in the First World War there was an appeal by George V for voluntary economy in food consumption. Many of the population of Colchester signed a pledge to do just that and sent it to the mayor. Cards with purple ribbons were displayed in the windows of houses following the pledge, which included nearly every house in the town.

A dinner for wounded soldiers in Colchester.

The military hospital, Colchester.

A famous local inhabitant of Tolleshunt D'Arcy was Sir Laming Worthington-Evans. He held several important government posts during the conflict, including at one point having control of munitions. Early in the war he was responsible for recruitment drives in the town and also started the Colchester Volunteers. This was a body of men who could not serve overseas for one reason or another. They were similar to the Home Guard of the Second World War and at the beginning only had one decent rifle between them. Worthington-Evans himself was responsible for drilling them, which he did at Land Lane Football Ground.

Although there was a military hospital in the town, it was not big enough for the number of military patients. The county hospital therefore started to take soldiers as patients. In 1914 half of the hundred beds were given over to the military. Women and children patients were transferred to the former girls' high school to make room for the soldiers. Huts were also built in the grounds as extra wards and added another 150 beds.

The town council did much for the soldiers posted there. There were numerous clubs and rest halls for the use of soldiers when off duty. These were based in church schools, the YMCA and other public buildings. The council published a booklet showing all thirty-five clubs with a map showing their locations. There were also two clubs for soldiers' wives where they could meet and discuss the effects on family life of their husbands being away on active duty.

A group of soldiers in Colchester during the First World War.

Sobraon Barracks, Colchester.

Sobraon Barracks, Colchester, with men drilling.

It was not only the army that did important war work. Even the boy scouts were enlisted to patrol telegraph wires at night because of the worries about enemy aliens. The boys were supported by older residents who would come out to bring them hot drinks.

As the war dragged on food supplies became scarcer, mainly because of the success of German U-boats in sinking supply ships. One of the problems in Colchester was the increased amount of food needed for not only the population but also the large garrison. The council formed a food control committee. Often crowds of up to 1,000 would gather to await supplies. There were often suspicions that the rich residents of the town were getting a bigger share of what was available. On one occasion there was a demonstration by mothers with infants in prams that led to the mayor himself becoming involved in selling them half-pound measures of margarine.

The supply of food to the public was seen to be fairer once ration cards were issued. The cards were administered by primary school teachers, who were given days off school to fill out the cards for the local population.

By 1918 there were still worries about invasion. Colchester was on alert and the population prepared to evacuate the area, destroying anything the enemy could use. The plan was to leave the town as barren as a desert for any invasion force. Families were given cards showing routes they should take if they needed to evacuate. As the roads needed to be clear for troops, these routes were mainly across country.

As well as the invasion fears, there was also a serious Spanish flu outbreak in the same year. Many died, no doubt partly owing to weakness from lack of a decent diet. The dead included many civilians as well as soldiers.

The camp church at Colchester in 1916.

Hyderabad Barracks, Colchester, with men marching.

The Cavalry Barracks, Colchester.

Colchester Garrison Gymnasium during the First World War.

The war memorial and castle at Colchester.

The county hospital treated over 4,000 soldiers during the war, and the council decided that adding a block to the building might be a fitting memorial. Although some money was budgeted for this, the rising cost of building made its completion impossible.

Despite the good work of the hospital the number of dead was colossal. Over 1,200 men from Colchester died during the war, which was many times the number in other towns with a similar population.

HARWICH

The town was transformed into a fortress during the First World War. Although restricted areas were common in the Second World War, Harwich was unusually restricted to strangers during the First World War as well. The town did not suffer as much from the Zeppelin and bomber attacks as those towns further south. This was because the enemy aircraft used the Thames as a clear route to the capital and passed over those towns on the Thames estuary. Being a seaport, however, Harwich was involved with German U-boats actions, especially as it was again used to transport troops and other goods to the Continent.

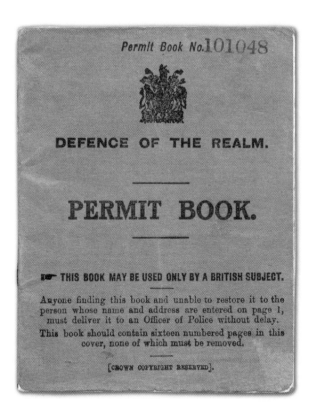

Permit Book No.101048

DEFENCE OF THE REALM.

PERMIT BOOK.

☞ THIS BOOK MAY BE USED ONLY BY A BRITISH SUBJECT.

Anyone finding this book and unable to restore it to the person whose name and address are entered on page 1, must deliver it to an Officer of Police without delay. This book should contain sixteen numbered pages in this cover, none of which must be removed.

[CROWN COPYRIGHT RESERVED].

A permit book to allow access to the Harwich Military Area. Although there were many restricted areas in the Second World War Harwich was also restricted during the First World War.

One famous event of the war connected with Harwich was the death of Captain Charles Fryatt. Fryatt was captain of a Great Eastern steamship, the *Brussels*, and in 1916 he rammed a German U-boat that had been watching his ship. On his next crossing, Fryatt was taken prisoner by the Germans and shot. The event was a disaster for German propaganda. Fryatt's body was returned to Essex and buried in Dovercourt.

At the end of the nineteenth century it had been decided to build a new type of defensive position at Beacon Hill Fort. The advances made in naval gunnery had made large visible forts much more vulnerable to the powerful and accurate guns aboard modern warships. The new battery was therefore armed with guns that were run out to fire and then returned into pits for reloading. The weapons in the new defences were much more sophisticated than those that had armed the redoubt.

Further defences were added at Beacon Hill Fort during the First World War. The original guns were replaced and more modern weapons added. The redoubt was again used by the military. It had been in use as barracks since 1910.

At the end of the war the port had some degree of revenge for the suffering the German U-boats had caused its shipping. It was agreed that all German U-boats would surrender to Admiral Tyrwhitt at Harwich. They came in with a supply ship, which was then used to take their crews back to Germany. By the end of 1918 there were 120 German U-boats lined up in the harbour. They were all sold for scrap.

A small silk, a precursor of cigarette cards, of the HMS Essex *from the First World War.*

The Ganges *Naval Training Ship off Harwich.*

A floating U-boat harbour at the port of Harwich after the German surrender.

U-boats off Harwich after the German surrender. The terms of the Armistice required Germany to turn over all U-boats to the British. Most of these were taken into custody at the port of Harwich.

More than 2,000 British merchant ships were destroyed by German U-boats in the First World War.

HORNCHURCH

In 1914, at the outbreak of the First World War, Hornchurch, despite its profitable past, was still just a small village close to Romford and surrounded by countryside, but it was not long after the outbreak of hostilities before the face of the village had changed completely. Every spare piece of land in the county seemed to become an army camp during the conflict, so it was no wonder that Hornchurch also changed.

The first army unit to arrive was the 3rd East Anglian, Howitzer, Brigade of the Royal Field Artillery. The officers set a precedent by staying at the White Hart Inn, while the men stayed in the school in North Street. They left their guns at Drury Falls. The unit was only in the village a few weeks, but they were just the first of many military forces that stayed.

In November of the same year the 1st Sportsman's Battalion arrived in the village. It was the first time that the village had been the site of an army barracks.

The battalion travelled by train from Liverpool Street to Hornchurch and then marched from the station to their new home at Grey Towers, a large house close to the centre of the village. Wooden huts had already been erected in the grounds. The locals came out in force to welcome the new residents. Patriotism seems to have been much more evident in this war than it had been in the fight against Napoleon.

The Sportsman Battalion was a unit that allowed older men to join. To qualify for membership the applicant had to have a skill in some form of sport or entertainment. The 2nd Sportsman's Battalion was posted close by at Hare Hall

Camp in Romford. They were later replaced at the camp by the Artists' Rifles, another unit that was made up of the talented young men of the population.

What seems a strange idea now, that of having army units made up of men with similar skills, was quite common at the time of the First World War. As well as the Artists there were also such units as the Post Office Rifles and the Civil Service Rifles. The well-publicised deaths of famous war poets in the Artists' Rifles are well documented but that was later in the war. When the first units of the Artists went to France, they were almost completely wiped out. The loss to the country of talented young men must have been catastrophic. The same was later true of the sporting stars and entertainers of the Sportsman's Battalion.

The village was transformed by the arrival of so many new faces. A rest room where the soldiers could meet with the locals was opened at the rear of the Baptist Church Hall in North Street. There was a very close relationship between the villagers and the soldiers. Concerts were put on at the camp, often in aid of local charities. The battalion even produced its own weekly magazine, the *Sportsman's Gazette*, while based in Hornchurch. The men would often march through the town to the railway station, led by a band.

This close relationship was evident at Christmas 1914 when locals left their homes on Christmas Day to join festivities in the huts at the camp. At 9.30 on Sunday mornings, the soldiers would march to St Andrew's Church for a service. The Sportsmen were not, however, to be based in the village for long. They left the

Grey Towers House, the site of Grey Towers Camp.

The Sportsman's Battalion arriving at Hornchurch.

peaceful Essex countryside in June the following year and went off to less welcoming parts. A brass plaque was placed in St Andrew's Church in Hornchurch as a memorial to the 769 men of the battalion who left Hornchurch for France and never returned.

The next soldiers to arrive at Grey Towers were the Middlesex Regiment. They were known as the Navvies Battalion, and were more of a manual labour than a fighting unit. They never had the level of local involvement that the Sportsmen had. They held their own church service on the parade ground with a band and their mascot, which was a goat.

One change that occurred in Hornchurch during their stay was a rise in crime. Private Henry Johnston of the Middlesex Regiment based at Hornchurch was sentenced to six weeks' hard labour for stealing a bicycle from Arthur Burrell of London Road, Romford, in October 1915.

The men who replaced them in January 1916 must have seemed even more unusual to the locals. They were from New Zealand and had several Maori soldiers with them. Grey Towers was the first base camp for New Zealand soldiers in Britain.

The first arrivals were mainly wounded men from hospitals, as the camp had become a convalescent hospital where they could recover before returning to action. There were soldiers from all units and to help them recover there were good recreational facilities at the camp, including several allotments where they could grow food for themselves.

THE SPORTSMAN'S BATTALION.

(SANCTIONED BY LORD KITCHENER.)

Finance Committee:
E. CUNLIFFE OWEN, C.M.G.
STANLEY HOLMES.
F. L. RAWSON, M.I.E.E., A.M.I.C.E.
Captain F. B. L. VAUGHAN.

Organizing Secretary:
E. CUNLIFFE OWEN (Mrs.)

INDIAN ROOM.
HOTEL CECIL.
STRAND, LONDON.

Dear Sir,

May we venture to interest you in the SPORTSMAN'S BATTALION now being raised? It has been accepted by Lord Kitchener, and will prove a unique part of his new Army for Active Service at the Front.

The strength of the BATTALION will be 1100, and will consist of hard, keen men of fine physique enured to outdoor life, good shots, and all keen sportsmen, whose sole aim and object is to serve King and Country.

Recruiting for this Battalion is nearly completed and the Medical Examination and Attestation by the War Office is now in progress.

In accordance with the order sanctioning its being raised the Battalion has to be HOUSED, EQUIPPED and FED by the Committee until it is taken over by the Government. We, as the Finance Committee, will feel most grateful to you if you will kindly do all in your power to help us to collect Funds to meet the expenses.

Sir William Plender, of Deloitte, Plender, Griffiths & Co. Chartered Accountants, has consented to act as Honorary Treasurer. Every care will be taken to ensure the proper disposal of Funds entrusted to us, and a full Financial Statement will in due course be forwarded to each subscriber.

Full details of the expenses which have to be incurred are appended, together with the sums to be refunded by the War Office under the Schedule of Regulations applying to this Battalion.

As the Battalion goes into training quarters during the week commencing the 12th inst., and there still remains a great deal to be done before that time, we shall be very grateful if you will do all in your power to assist us as speedily and liberally as possible.

Thanking you in anticipation for your kind and generous help.

We are,

Yours faithfully,

On behalf of the Committee,

E. Cunliffe-Owen.

Organizing Secretary.

Above: *A letter sent out to raise money for the Sportsman's Battalion.* (C. Chaloner)

THE SPORTSMAN'S BATTALION

ROYAL FUSILIERS.

(SANCTIONED BY LORD KITCHENER.)

INDIAN ROOM,
HOTEL CECIL,
STRAND, LONDON.

TAKE THIS NOTICE WITH YOU.

Sir,

You should proceed to nearest Military Barracks or Recruiting Office and ask to be Medically examined and attested for the Royal Fusiliers on A.F.B. 2065.

If passed fit and up to standard height, 5ft. 6in., chest 35½in. (age up to 45), you will be despatched under Warrant to the Sportsman's Battalion Royal Fusiliers.

You will report yourself at above address at 11 a.m. on October 14th.

Thomas Whiffen Captain,
Captain R.
Recruiting Staff Officer.
Recruiting Staff Officer.

Left: *A call-up letter for the Sportsman's Battalion.* (C. Chaloner)

Men of the Sportsman's Battalion at Grey Towers gates in the snow.

As with the Sportsman's Battalion, there was plenty of contact with the locals. Perhaps the strangest display the people of Hornchurch were treated to was the famous Haka performed by twenty Maori warriors. They were part of the surviving 100 men out of 500 Maoris who had gone to fight at Gallipoli. A pantomime was put on by the soldiers at the camp in December 1916, Ali Baba and the more or less forty thieves.

Some New Zealanders were billeted in local homes. Although rationing was not as widespread during the first war as it was in the second, there were still shortages, and when the New Zealand soldiers worked in the local fields, laying telephone wires, they would often bring home vegetables they found growing there. They were a welcome addition to the family food supply, if not quite legal.

Not all of the men who had come so far returned to their homes. Many died and were buried in France, but some of the Maoris were buried in St Andrew's churchyard in Hornchurch. One of the windows in the church displays the arms of New Zealand commemorating the base at Grey Towers.

The soldiers from the camp played a big part in village life. There were many balls and concerts both in the village and the camp. The cinema in Station Lane was used by the soldiers. It had opened in 1913 with the original name of the Hornchurch Cinema. Later it became the first Queen's Theatre.

Apart from the church window, the soldiers from New Zealand left another memento, a meeting house where they used to relax. Originally it was a hut in

Grey Towers camp under snow in the winter of 1914.

Soldiers waiting for a train at Hornchurch station.

A Stereoview of the Sportsman's Battalion leaving Hornchurch for the final time.

Hornchurch, but then a more permanent building was erected in Butts Green Road to house the club. The building is still there and is a now private residence.

Grey Towers has gone and the grounds are now covered by housing. A new cinema opened in 1935 close to the site of the old house and was called the Towers after the old house. It later became a bingo hall. The present Grey Towers Avenue used to be the driveway up to the house.

The interior of a hut at Grey Towers Camp, Hornchurch.

Hamilton Avenue at Grey Towers while it was a New Zealand Forces convalescent camp.

Station Road, Hornchurch, which led to Sutton's Farm and the aerodrome.

A little further up the road from the village, something else happened as a result of the war. Tom Crawford, who had farmed Sutton's Farm for years, had part of his land requisitioned by the government for an airfield.

The almost unhindered bombing of the south-east of the country by German Zeppelins was forcing the government to do something to combat the menace. Although the use of aeroplanes as weapons of war was still very new, the construction of an airfield at Hornchurch was part of a widespread attempt to stop the bombing.

There were plans to set up a series of airfields along the coast as a system of defence against air attacks. Because of their unreliability and the short distance the aeroplanes of the time could manage to fly, the plan was to have airfields no more than thirty miles apart. Fields were set up at Stow Maries, Goldhanger, North Weald and Rochford. Many only had two planes to begin with but by 1918 Rochford had eight.

Zeppelins soon became a common sight in the skies over Hornchurch as they made their way towards London. At night they were lit up by the searchlights that had been placed around the area.

Although aeroplanes were not a common sight, the people of Hornchurch must have had some experience of the strange machines. Six years previously the *Barking, East Ham & Ilford Advertiser* had run the headline 'Monsters of the air at

Page 221   *The War Illustrated, 21st October, 1915.*

With the Royal Flying Corps Zeppelin Strafers

Sec.-Lieut. F. Sowrey, awarded the
D.S.O. for attack on a Zeppelin.

Group of R.F.C. officers arm-in-arm, including
Lieut. Robinson and Lieut. Sowrey.

Lieut. Brandon, awarded D.S.O.
for attacking enemy air-craft.

BOTH on the west front and at home have our aviators established permanent ascendancy over the enemy. The fact that four Zeppelins have been brought down in England may induce the Germans to modify their policy of frightfulness, in spite of the ravings of Count Zeppelin.

This notorious German must find it increasingly difficult to justify his hideous invention, and one which has cost his Fatherland several millions—to no real military purpose.

It is significant that where competent German reconnaissance is most needed, on the Somme front, it is conspicuously unsuccessful. Certainly no Zeppelin dare appear over the Franco-British line, for it would be immediately riddled with shells. That is why Paris is immune from the couriers of hate, and, no doubt, with the perfection of London defences the Zeppelin will find it increasingly dangerous to approach the British metropolis.

Lieut. Robinson's squadron I of the Royal Flying Corps on
parade at headquarters.

Mark of the Hun! Would-be baby-killer who jumped from
Zeppelin at Potter's Bar left this mark on the turf.

Brother heroes of the R.F.C. Left to right: Lieut. Robinson, V.C.,
Lieut. Tempest, and Sec.-Lieut. Sowrey, D.S.O.

Group of RFC officers, including Robinson and Sowrey.

Leefe Robinson's Zeppelin coming down in flames.

ZEPPELIN BROUGHT DOWN IN FLAMES
AT CUFFLEY, NEAR ENFIELD, AT 2.30 A.M., SUNDAY SEPT 3rd 1916.

Dagenham'. The headline was related to a site set up by the Aeronautical Society of Great Britain in the marshes at Dagenham next to the Thames. It was the first flying ground in England. Although it did not last long, other early aviators also flew over the area when in 1913 there was an air derby around London, one of the turning points being at West Thurrock.

The aeroplanes arrived in October 1915. There were two Royal Aircraft Factory BE2c biplanes and two pilots from the Royal Flying Corps (RFC). Everything about the airfield was temporary. The hangars were made of canvas; the ground crew were billeted in local houses while the pilots stayed at the White Hart Hotel in the village. The number of pilots increased over the next few weeks.

Although it was easy enough for the pilots to find the Zeppelins as they came across the channel, there was not much they could do to stop them, as the ammunition the aeroplanes used had little effect. The first Zeppelin to be brought down by an aeroplane was the L15. Damaged by explosive darts by a pilot from Hainault airfield, the Zeppelin finally came down in the sea off Margate.

By September 1916 the number of aircraft at Hornchurch had increased to six and the hangars were by then made of timber. One of the new pilots was Lieutenant

Leefe Robinson. With his guns loaded with the new explosive-type bullets invented by John Pomeroy, he came across a Zeppelin near Woolwich. The bullets set the airship alight and its demise was visible over much of Essex as it crashed in flames at Cuffley near Enfield. It was the first airship to be brought down over the mainland.

The wreck became a tourist attraction and Leefe Robinson became an overnight celebrity. His photograph was printed in the newspapers and in magazines. In the local *Barking, East Ham & Ilford Advertiser*, it was reported that the burning Zeppelin was seen by thousands of people throughout Essex. The paper also printed reports from witnesses in Romford and in Epping. Within days Leefe Robinson was awarded the Victoria Cross at Windsor Castle by King George V.

Leefe Robinson became one of the most famous men in the country overnight, and sightseers would turn up at the airfield hoping to see him. But fame and a medal were not his only rewards. A cash reward for the first Zeppelin to be shot down over the mainland had been offered and Leefe Robinson got it. Out of the money he bought a car, which were as rare a sight in the area as the aeroplanes he flew. A few weeks after his success, Robinson was taking off in the same plane he had used when

Above: *Lieutenant Leefe Robinson showing his Victoria Cross.*

Left: *Going, Going, Gone. A card celebrating Robinson's victory.*

The wreckage of Leefe Robinson's Zeppelin at Cuffley.

shooting down the Zeppelin when he crashed on take-off. The plane was totally destroyed.

Leefe Robinson's feat was soon to be repeated, and strangely two more pilots from Hornchurch also shot down Zeppelins. These were Lieutenant Sowrey and Lieutenant Tempest. After Sowrey shot down his, all three men raced through the village in Robinson's car late one night on their way to Billericay to see the wreckage. Sowrey and Tempest both received the DSO. The local residents presented each with a silver cup at the Grey Towers camp in October 1916.

Leefe Robinson left Hornchurch and went to France where he was shot down and captured. After a long period as a prisoner of war he returned home, but his health had suffered during his captivity. He died shortly after from Spanish flu.

It was not long before the Zeppelins were replaced by German planes. This led to the first dogfights between aircraft over the town as the aircraft from Sutton's Farm tried to stop the enemy planes from reaching London. With the number of air raids diminishing, a sports day was held at Sutton's Farm. It was the first public open day at the airfield, and it became a regular event later in the field's life, which was also to include flying displays. That was much later, however. In 1919 the airfield was closed down as there seemed no more need for it.

However, in 1924 it was decided that Sutton's Farm would reopen as an airbase. The government had realised the value of the aeroplane as a means of defence.

PURFLEET

Conditions for the soldiers at Purfleet must have improved at the camp over time, as a new canteen had been built in 1873. For the first few years it was run by tenants who were all ex-army men. It was then taken over by the Middlesex Regiment, who ran it until the man they put in charge was involved in some financial irregularities. He committed suicide by drowning himself in the Thames close to the Royal Hotel. The canteen was then run on the tenant system until the First World War.

Apart from the magazine Purfleet had other associations with the army. During a dock strike the Argyll and Sutherland Highlanders were sent to the area to guard against riots. The area was also used to train recruits in the First World War, when trenches were dug to resemble those on the Somme. Units from other camps in the area were brought in to use the training facilities. Even so, this practical arrangement could in no way have prepared them for the horrors of the real thing when they arrived at the trenches in France.

It would seem that the Purfleet site had been prepared to be used for troop movements, and transport to the area had been updated before the war began. In 1910 a signal box was added to serve a new halt and sidings close to the magazine. The halt and box were called Purfleet Rifle Range Box.

In 1915 one of the famous war poets of the First World War was based at nearby Romford. Edward Thomas was a member of the Artists' Rifles officer training school at Hare Hall. It is possible that he visited Purfleet, as it was used for training many regiments.

While based in Romford, Thomas wrote a number of poems that were influenced by the local areas. One that he wrote in 1915 was called 'The Chalk-Pit'. It could be that the inspiration for the poem was the chalk cliffs of Purfleet.

Purfleet Village, pre-First World War. The magazine is behind the bushes.

A view from the river with the Royal Hotel in the centre and the magazine to the left.

'Souvenir of the Great War'. This card was issued by the London Electrical Engineers based at Purfleet.

ROMFORD

The beginning of the First World War did not have much impact on the Romford area. The war did not even make the front page of the local newspaper. 'Why we went to war' was an article on the second page next to the football results. The seriousness of the situation only hit home when the town began to fill with soldiers.

It had long been a tradition that soldiers were billeted in inns or schools, or put up in private homes. Therefore, in August 1914, billeting officers visited Romford house-holders to check available accommodation. Even the princely sum of 2s 9d a day per man did not persuade everyone that taking a soldier into their home was a good idea.

One of the army units to be closely connected with the area had already visited a few months earlier. Fifty non-commissioned officers and men of the Artists' Rifles, A company, visited Ingatestone for a weekend. Captain Passmore-Edwards, a member of a family with very strong connections with the East End of London, commanded them.

The outbreak of war soon began to have an effect on local life. The closing time for pubs and clubs was changed to an earlier 10 p.m. By the end of 1914 invasion fears were rife and a meeting to discuss the situation was held at the Romford Corn Exchange in December. It was chaired by Sir Montague Turner and included Sir John Bethell MP. At the well-attended meeting it was stated that the people of Britain were fighting for their very existence.

The roll of honour in the local press named the men from the area who had so far died in the conflict. It steadily lengthened as the war continued. The conflict also

Hare Street was a quiet village before the army invaded it.

Hare Hall in the mid-nineteenth century. The Hall became the officers' quarters at Hare Hall Camp.

reached out to Romford when a guard at Romford railway station sighted a Zeppelin in May. It flew over at 3 a.m. and was visible for half an hour.

Although there was no damage in the area from enemy action, some was caused by soldiers billeted in the town. Tudor House in Reed Pond Walk, the property of the Gidea Park Estate Company that had begun to build large houses in the area, was being used as a billet for fifty men of the King's Royal Rifles. As they got ready to leave, a fire started in one of the bedrooms and gutted the building.

Hare Hall in Gidea Park became the home of the Artists' Rifles after being occupied by other units. Sir Herbert Raphael, who formerly lived nearby at Gidea Hall, served as a private in the second Sportsman's Battalion, which was due to stay at the Hare Hall camp on a temporary basis. The rumour that they were coming went on for so long that when they finally did arrive, looking very smart with white gloves tucked under their shoulder straps, no one paid much attention. About 1,000 men were led from Gidea Park station to the camp commanded by Colonel Paget. Sir Herbert was not in the ranks as he was suffering from a heavy cold.

Hare Hall camp had room for around 1,200 men. The Hall had been the residence of Majors G. Castellan and Victor Castellan, who were both serving with the Royal Artillery.

The presence of so many extra men in the area increased the number of local events. The soldiers held several sports days, and Lady Raphael presented prizes at a

The Artists' Rifles sports day at Hare Hall Camp.

cross-country run at Gidea Park organised by the 18th King's Royal Rifles. In the town itself the YMCA building proved too small for the numbers of new arrivals and was transferred to the Wykham Hall next to St Edward's Church, but when that also proved too small, it was transferred to the Corn Exchange.

The influx of so many young men also brought an increase in crime levels. Miss Amy Paterson, a teacher of Eastern Road, had befriended a Private Bernard Towes of the Royal Fusiliers stationed at Hare Hall. He then stole a coat and a gold watch and chain from her and sold the watch at Porritt's pawnbrokers in High Street. Towes was sent for trial at the Essex Quarter Sessions.

But the effects of the soldiers' arrival on the local female population were not all bad. In August 1916 there was a wedding at St Edward's Church in Romford marketplace. Captain Harold Trim from Wimbledon married Mary Elizabeth Laura Tedon of Laureate, Como Street, Romford. The Revd H.B. Curtis, Chaplain of the Hare Hall Camp, performed the ceremony.

Hare Hall was one of the main camps in Romford. The hall was on the site of an older house known as Godwins that was built in 1768–9 by John Wallenger, now commemorated in the name of Wallenger Avenue. It was enlarged in 1896. The Hall stood in Hare Street, which was part of what is now Main Road, starting from Balgores Lane going eastward.

When the war broke out Hare Street was a small country hamlet just outside Romford with a few shops and inns and some cottages. The well-known landscape gardener and artist Humphrey Repton had lived on the corner of Hare Street and

Balgores Lane. He had been responsible for designing the gardens of Gidea Hall, part of which became Raphael's Park. He also designed many other gardens across the country.

The 2nd Battalion of the Artists' Rifles came to Hare Hall and were followed by the 3rd Battalion. They were part of the 28th London Regiment, a territorial force that had come together as a result of a merger of the old militia and volunteers. In 1848 many rifle companies were formed in response to the danger caused by the revolutions in Europe. These consisted mainly of men from the middle classes. Other units within the 28th London Regiment were the Post Office Rifles and the Civil Service Rifles.

The 1st Battalion of the Artists' Rifles had been to France and suffered terrible casualties. Mr Tweedy Smith, the prospective Liberal candidate for Maldon, had a son Alan who was serving with the Artists' Rifles. Some of his letters from the front were printed in the *Barking, East Ham & Ilford Advertiser*. Alan was later killed in action.

The 2nd and 3rd Battalions of the Rifles had then become an officer training corps. It took about thirteen weeks to train an officer, and commanding officers from other regiments would come to the camp to pick the best men for their units.

The officers in charge of the camp lived in Hare Hall, while the men lived in large wooden barracks that they had built in the grounds. As the camp grew, Sir Henry Raphael offered them the use of Gidea Hall and Balgores House, which until then had been the home of the Golf Club secretary.

A field kitchen and the wagons used to carry it in Romford in 1916. It was no doubt used to feed the many army units based in the town.

In other parts of Romford troops were billeted in school buildings and often camped in the grounds as well. Hare Street changed from a quiet hamlet to a bustling village. There had already been expansion in the area with the building of the Gidea Park Garden Suburb in 1910. Humphrey Cook, the military tailors, took over one of the shops in Hare Street. The Premier coffee house, which had until then mainly been used by walkers from Romford, now became very busy with soldiers. Nearby Raphael's Park was also well used by the men when off duty.

The Artist Rifles consisted of men from all walks of life. The best known were two of the famous war poets of the First World War, Wilfred Owen and Edward Thomas. When joining the Rifles, Owen was said to be surprised to find that there were no artists, although actually there were. One of them was John Nash, the well-known war artist, who had been with the 1st Battalion of the Artists' Rifles in France and was one of the few survivors. Another was William Robinson, who described them as a mixture of lawyers, journalists and some artists. Owen and Thomas were stationed at Hare Hall and both went on to die in France, Owen in the final week of the conflict.

Wilfred Owen came from a middle-class family that had fallen on hard times. He had been a teacher and a clergyman's assistant before joining the army. He helped to build the huts at Hare Hall and wrote a postcard to a friend saying how he 'slaved from 6.30 am to 6.30 pm in their construction'.

Owen left Hare Hall to take up a commission in the Manchester Regiment as a second lieutenant. He suffered from shell shock but went on to win the Military Cross. His poems were not published until after his death.

Edward Thomas was already a writer before the war, but had achieved no real fame. He was known as a poet of the English countryside, and many of his poems and his earlier writings convey his love of nature. Despite his love of the countryside, he was in fact born in London and only experienced the countryside on boyhood holidays in South Wales. Unlike Owen, many of his poems were influenced by his time at Hare Hall.

Thomas's poems were commonly interpreted as thoughts of the peace of the English countryside while in the hell of the trenches. The problem with this view is that he wrote his poetry before he went to France. Thomas was 36 and married with children before he enlisted. His first posting with the Rifles was at High Beech in Epping, and while he was there his family lived nearby. Later he transferred to Hare Hall where he was a lance corporal instructing officers. In his ten months' stay there he wrote over forty poems. In 1916 he was commissioned into the Royal Artillery and was killed at Arras on Easter Monday 1917.

The poems that he wrote while at Epping, where his family lived, and Romford, were often influenced by the countryside around him, and many were written for his family. In his poem 'Myfanwy' he mentions South Weald, Havering and Havering atte Bower. There is no doubt that many of the features that he describes in his other poems were also from the local area.

Gidea Hall is gone now but Hare Hall has survived. Three years after the war it became the Liberty Grammar School. Over the years more modern extensions have been added to the old Hall, but the rear is largely original. It is now the Royal

Liberty School in Upper Brentwood Road. Balgores House where Thomas stayed still exists and is a nursery school. It is now difficult to imagine that the area was once a large army camp.

SHOEBURYNESS

By the end of the nineteenth century the artillery had been split into two sections: the Royal Field Artillery and the Royal Garrison Artillery. The Shoeburyness site was only involved in the Garrison side and mainly concentrated on naval weapons.

The improvement in weapons aboard modern warships was not always matched by an improvement in naval skills. In 1905 the battleship *King Alfred* became stranded on Shoebury Sands, and it was not the only large warship to run aground in Essex.

Shoeburyness's first cinema opened just before the war. The Picture Palace could hold 350 people, and many of its patrons were probably soldiers.

The beginning of the First World War led to major changes at the camp. Units were sent from Shoebury to other areas, such as Purfleet, to protect the magazine from air attack. The Border Regiment was posted at Shoeburyness to protect against sabotage and invasion. Many other units were drafted into the area, including the Rifle Brigade, which was billeted in the Kursaal at Southend. The camp theatre was converted into a hospital. The influx of troops led to a shift in the relaxed attitude of the locals towards the army. There were numerous outbreaks of violence involving

The west gate at Shoeburyness Barracks, pre-First World War.

the new military arrivals. These consisted of fights between regiments as well as military against civilians.

In 1916 King George V visited Shoeburyness to inspect the new ranges. Foulness Island had been purchased by the government the previous year. Along with other established military bases, Shoeburyness became a transit camp for soldiers on their way to the trenches in France.

Although no attack was made on the Shoeburyness site by enemy aircraft, they often passed overhead. A few bombs were dropped on the town itself but there was little damage, while nearby Southend, with no real military establishments, suffered several air raids from both Zeppelins and planes. Like other military sites on the Thames, Shoebury lay on the route that German airmen took on their way to London. No lives were lost from enemy action, but there were fatalities from accidents in firing guns. Captain Lane Poole was killed in 1915 and five men died in 1917. Also in the same year a large fire started in the ranges that led to the evacuation of the whole town. The Kursaal at Southend was used to shelter the evacuees.

A hut caught light and the fire began to set off the shells stored there. The fire spread and shells continued to explode for twenty-four hours, including many of those stored on railway wagons. Although only one life was lost, the loss of ammunition needed for the war effort was a very serious setback.

Following the tradition of keeping the production of explosive materials out of the way on the bank of the Thames, a factory had been built in 1895 further along the river on the marshes stretching from Stanford-le-Hope to Holehaven Creek. It

The garrison church at Shoeburyness.

The clock tower, Shoeburyness, 1909.

A military band by the clock tower, Shoeburyness, 1916.

A military camp at Shoeburyness in the First World War.

was built by Kynoch and Company and employed over 600 workers in making explosives for the South African war. It had its own school and shop and became known as Kynochtown. It continued production throughout the First World War and finally closed in 1919, after which it became an oil refinery.

WARLEY

Warley had replaced Colchester as the centre of the county regiment but they were often not based at the barracks. While the Essex Regiment was abroad, as they often were, other visiting regiments took over the barracks. These would then move on to France and be replaced by others. During the First World War some of the Guards regiments were based there. In 1914 the Prince of Wales came to Warley to enlist in the Grenadier Guards.

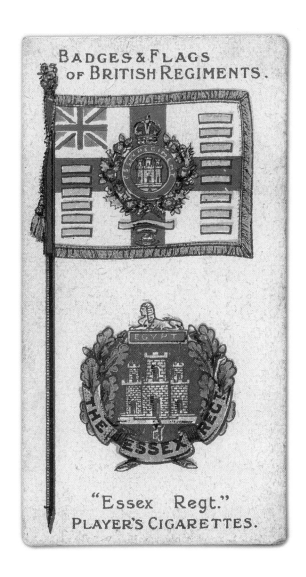

A cigarette card showing the Essex regimental badge and colours.

A military band entering Warley Barracks, pre-First World War.

IN LOVING MEMORY

A card mourning the death of Sergeant Rene Burwood, killed in France in 1916. The card shows how young many of the soldiers who died in the war must have been. Burwood was only 21 but was already a sergeant.

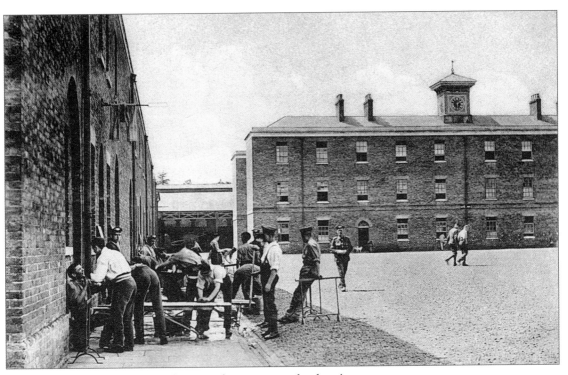

Warley Barracks. The men in the central area seem to be cleaning.

The front of Warley Barracks.

An Essex Regiment soldier and his wife, pictured during the First World War.

The introduction of rationing opened up opportunities for the less honest men among the residents of Warley. A lot of black market dealing went on between the soldiers and the local population during the First World War. In the *Barking, East Ham & Ilford Advertiser* there was a report about several men who bought items from soldiers at the barracks and ended up in court. Ernest Brown of Brook Street was fined twenty shillings for buying two cardigan jackets from a soldier. At the same hearing John Ouley, also of Brook Street, was fined half a crown for unlawfully receiving two blankets and an overcoat from soldiers from the camp. A soldier, private Thomas Bradbury, was remanded in custody for stealing five 1lb packs of butter, some of which he had made into parcels and addressed ready to be posted.

THREE

The Second World War to the Present Day

The Second World War was the third and last occasion that Essex became an armed camp in response to invasion fears. It was the greatest threat yet and was met with more men and equipment than ever before. Also greater numbers of men from other countries poured into Essex than had in previous conflicts.

After the retreat from Dunkirk the British Army was seriously short of weapons and equipment, much of which had been abandoned on the French beaches. This shortage was most obvious in Essex, where the guns deployed along the coast were of vintage stock, often from the First World War or even before. Many of these defences were manned by Home Guard units.

Many areas around the coast became closed to non-residents, and later there were efforts to remove all civilians. As well as restrictions on movement, the residents had to face a level of air raids and rationing that was much more severe than in the First World War.

At first parts of Essex were used to house evacuees. There were three area categories, Evacuation, Neutral and Reception. Most evacuees who came to Essex were from London. But as the war went on, it became evident that such towns as Colchester, which had been a reception area, was just as dangerous as where the evacuees had come from, and children were evacuated again as Colchester became itself an evacuation area. Because of the constant danger from air raids, the Home Office issued an information book on what to do if your house was bombed.

Place names and road signs were removed in the county and the balance of the population changed as the young men went into the forces and the middle-aged into war work. The coastal resorts, which had hoped to have some level of summer seasons, became ghost towns, as the only visitors they were allowed were the troops posted to protect them.

The changes to the way of life in Essex towns were more pronounced than they had been during any other conflict. Enormous numbers of troops arrived, often from overseas. The population in towns like Colchester may have been used to the military presence, but these men were foreigners. The nearest thing to foreign troops they had seen before were the Scottish regiments who were stationed at Weeley and Maldon in the French wars.

A.R.P.

In accordance with our very progressive policy, we have investigated the possibilities of a small Air Raid Shelter, and have one constructed in our Showroom. We shall be very pleased to show this to anyone who may be interested.

Left: The civilian population was being prepared for war as this advertisement for air raid shelters from a pre-war football programme shows.

Right: The Blackout may have been meant to save lives but was not without its own dangers, as indicated by this road safety warning.

Above: An example of business cashing in on the war, a patriotic matchbox label.

Everyone in the country was forced to carry an identity card for the duration of the war.

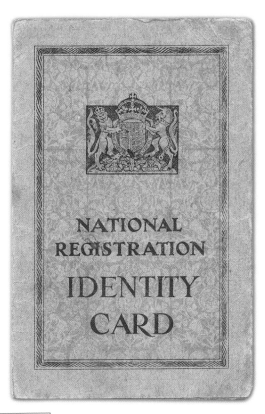

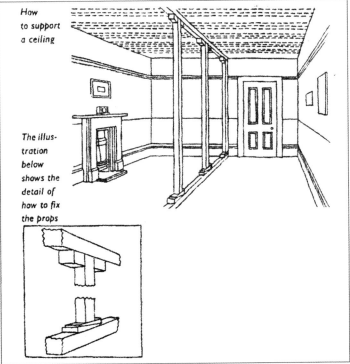

How to support a ceiling

The illustration below shows the detail of how to fix the props

How to strengthen your room. A diagram from a Home Office booklet on protecting homes against air raids. (HMSO)

A postwar group of officers and men from several different regiments in Romford with a trophy awarded for shooting.

The Burnston Home Guard outside the Spotted Dog public house near Great Dunmow. (Essex Record Office)

The 1st Battalion Essex Home Guard. The battalion had an exciting time during grenade practice at Thorpe Hall Golf Course in 1941. One of the men pulled the pin out and dropped the grenade, then ran away. Second Lieutentant S.J. White picked up the live grenade and threw it away from the men. (Essex Record Office)

During the Second World War there were numerous camps of various sizes throughout Essex. Many were small units where soldiers were set to guard some important institution or site. Often these regular soldiers would be supporting Home Guard units, especially at artillery and anti-aircraft sites.

There was a much stricter rationing regime than there had been in the First World War. The lack of food led to leaflets being published with recipes using the restricted number of ingredients that were available. Magazines even offered prizes for simple recipes. There was also the Blackout to contend with. Many people believed that this caused more deaths than it saved, because of road accidents and the increased probability of people losing their footing in the darkness.

AUDLEY END HOUSE

This is a building with large private grounds that dates back to the eighteenth century. During the Second World War it was offered to the government for military use by the owners but was turned down as unsuitable. However, when the house's

Audley End House.

owner Lord Braybrooke died in March 1941, the house was taken over by the military with very little notice for the occupants. For the early part of the war it was used as an army camp by several different regiments.

An event that was to have an effect on Audley End House occurred in 1940 when a secret meeting was held in Anthony Eden's office, and the decision was made to set up a Special Operations Executive (SOE). This supplied small units of men to work with resistance groups in occupied territories. Churchill asked Hugh Dalton, the Minister of Economic Warfare, to take charge. His experience of economic matters was useful as one of the SOE.'s functions was to pay Arab leaders in the Middle East to stay neutral. There is also a belief that General Franco in Spain stayed neutral because of such payments.

Although best known for contact with the French Resistance, by 1943 the SOE was also in contact with guerrilla groups in Albania and Yugoslavia. They negotiated with groups who were in dispute with each other and led attacks against the Germans and Italians. This often led to reprisals against the local population. Many of the men involved were English officers. One of the most famous was the writer Evelyn Waugh. Despite admitting that he was one of the worst officers in the army, he was a member of the SOE, the Commandos and the Special Air Service.

The invasion of Poland influenced what happened to Audley End House. Some units of the Polish Army refused to surrender to the Germans and ended up in Britain along with the exiled Polish government. Volunteers were called for to work in occupied Poland, and those chosen were sent for training at Station 43, as by then Audley End House had become an SOE school that was best known for housing Polish trainees. The men involved in special operations were not spies but soldiers who worked in many undercover situations. Those from Station 43 became responsible to the Polish resistance once they were dropped into the country, but those operating in other countries stayed under British control.

In Poland the operatives had to face both Germans and Russians, and they were usually involved some kind of sabotage to transport systems or such vital travel links as bridges.

The selection process for volunteers was very stiff, and even those chosen did not always succeed in the training. The instructors at Station 43 were also Polish. Only about a quarter of those men chosen eventually passed out and went on to take part in missions. Of those that did many did not survive, while others ended up as prisoners in German concentration camps.

As well as the Poles there were also British soldiers at the camp. Some of these were transferred from other Essex barracks and were often wounded or unfit for other duties. They took care of the running of the camp and were also responsible for guarding the grounds.

Although Station 43's use was a secret, it was hard to black out completely everything that was going on there. The local Home Guard took part in training sessions with the men from the camp, and other local military bases had an idea of what was going on, as did the local police. Otherwise they would have been continually investigating reports of strange events occurring at the house.

The site of Audley End House made the posting quite a pleasant experience for the men. The British soldiers and the instructors used the Forces' Club in nearby King's Street, Saffron Walden. It was also possible to supplement meagre rations with duck eggs and fish from the River Cam.

The station finally closed as an SOE base in 1944. It was then transferred to newly liberated Italy. This meant that the journey to occupied countries in Europe was much shorter.

CHELMSFORD

During the Second World War Chelmsford continued its long association with volunteer units. The 6th Essex Battalion was a Home Guard unit based in Springfield Hill. If the threatened invasion occurred, one of their tasks was to destroy the Esso petrol depot in Victoria Road. Chelmsford post office staff also played a large part in forming Home Guard units. The 35th GPO Battalion was formed in the town and commanded by the town's head postmaster, Lieutenant Colonel Gaze. The battalion had a strength of 650.

An anti-aircraft rocket projector manned by relief no. 5 of the Chelmsford Home Guard, 1943–4. (Essex Record Office)

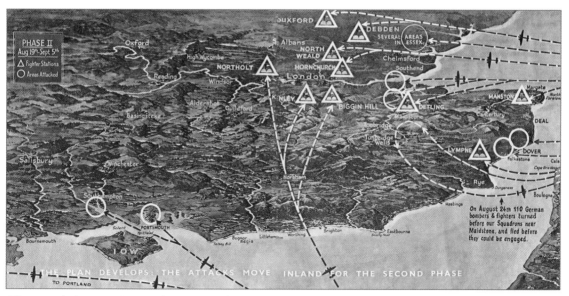

The second phase of air attacks, 19 August to 5 September 1940, when they finally reached Essex.
(HMSO, Battle of Britain Booklet)

Although it was used as an evacuation area for children from London at the outset of the war, it quickly became obvious that the town was itself a target for air raids, and an attempt was made to mislead enemy bombers by building a dummy town near Little Baddow. This was one of the best-kept secrets of the war along with other decoys to fool the bombers such as the dummy oil refineries on the Thames and even an imitation Air Force base. The airfield at North Weald was replicated at Nazing, using plywood Hurricanes from Shepperton Film Studios. It was believed that there were up to sixteen of these false sites in the county.

Chelmsford was perhaps the only town in Britain whose mayor, John Thompson, was killed in an air raid. Thompson had been in public life for many years and had also been mayor during the First World War. He was also part owner of the *Essex Chronicle* and used the newspaper to help launch a fund in the town to raise £15,000 to buy fighter planes for the RAF. Early in the war, however, Alderman Thompson's house was bombed, and he, his wife, his son and two grandchildren were killed.

German bombs often fell on Chelmsford and at times caused great loss of life. In 1944 shops in the high street were damaged and a suet factory burnt out. There was also damage to the prison. One of the most lethal attacks occurred when a V2 rocket landed on the town. Forty people were killed when the rocket struck close to the Hoffman ball bearing factory, which also made aircraft parts. It happened just before Christmas 1944, and earlier that day the staff had been singing Christmas carols with the Salvation Army. American servicemen based in the area were among the first to arrive and help the injured.

The Chelmsford Home Guard. (Essex Record Office)

The Marconi Company Home Guard. Many of the large factories in the county had their own Home Guard force. (Essex Record Office)

The American Forces commemorative window in the porchway of Chelmsford Cathedral.

It should be remembered that not only natives of Essex died defending our country. The American forces that also served are commemorated in a memorial in the south porch of Chelmsford Cathedral.

Chelmsford is still the site of the Essex Regiment Museum even though the regiment no longer exists. There is also a company of the East of England Regiment in the town. This is a reserve and cadets unit. The Essex Army Cadet Force run part-time courses including residential weekends and a longer yearly camp. The Essex Yeomanry Signal Squadron is a territorial unit also based in Chelmsford. They often serve with the regular army in trouble spots all over the world.

CHIGWELL

RAF Chigwell was unusual in that it was an RAF base without any planes. It had its origins in 1937 when the Balloon Training unit was started. The following year, before the war had even begun, Balloon Command was formed and the Essex Regiment drill hall in Chigwell was used as a recruitment centre for men to enlist in the new arm of the forces.

"Always something *wrong with this outfit!"*

Cartoon drawn by the camp commandant, Air Commodore B.C.H. Drew. (Jenny Filby)

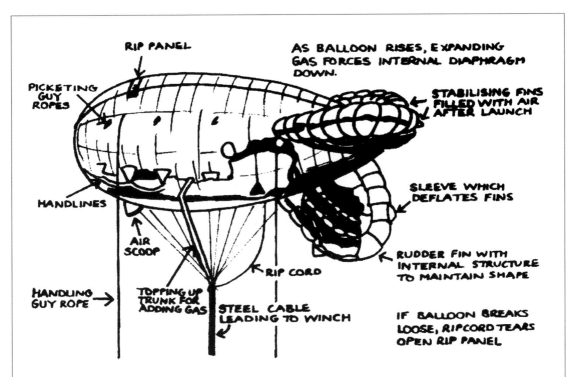

ANATOMY OF A BARRAGE BALLOON

Length	66ft
Diameter	18ft
Height	30ft
Material	600 separate pieces of Egyptian cotton, assembled on opposite bias and totalling 1000 sq. yds. material.
Cost	£500
Coating	"Dope" – a black rubber, waterproof undercoat, and an aluminium varnish top coat.
Gas	20,000 cu. ft. hydrogen per balloon; 60 cylinders required per launch; cost £50 per launch.

Anatomy of a barrage balloon. (Jenny Filby)

The aim of using the balloons was to deter dive-bombing and low-level attacks. This idea had originated in the First World War. Each balloon was connected to a winch, which enabled the crew to alter the height at which it flew. Pictures of the balloons in the night sky are one of the most memorable sights of the war. There were around 1,000 balloons positioned along the Thames alone.

In August 1938 a 70-acre site was set up in Chigwell as a balloon centre with large hangars and several huts. It was manned by both WAAFs (Women's Auxiliary Air Force) and airmen. There were three other centres which were also responsible for protecting the capital.

Because many of the personnel at the base had been recruited locally they were still allowed to live at home in the early days of the base. As so many from the base had local connections, it is no surprise that the base became very involved in the local community.

Metal hoops were screwed into the ground before the balloon was fixed to them and allowed to rise into the air. Some sites were permanent and had fixings already in place. The balloon crews would drive to the sites whenever there was an air raid warning.

The worst enemy of the balloon crews was the weather. High winds could lead to the balloon breaking away and flying off into the sky. A free-floating balloon could cause serious damage to anything, enemy or friendly. In one storm alone thirty-nine of Chigwell's balloons were destroyed.

After Dunkirk Chigwell was used to house many of the soldiers saved from the French beaches. The soldiers were given use of the huts while the base personnel moved into the hangars.

By 1942 air raids on London became less frequent, and this meant that there was less for balloon staff at Chigwell to do. By then the base had become a training centre, but many of those trained there found that they were quickly sent to do other jobs. There were fewer WAAFs employed in Balloon Command by this time.

By early in 1943 the use of balloons had declined even further and RAF Chigwell found itself changing roles. It became a training centre for mobile air traffic control groups who would be needed for the invasion the following year.

There are different views as to how effective barrage balloons were. Some believe that they actually brought down as many of our own aircraft as they did of the enemy's. Of course it is hard to measure their effectiveness as a deterrent. One thing that is not in dispute is that they were responsible for bringing down a number of the V1 flying bombs, the doodlebugs.

COALHOUSE FORT

During the Second World War the fort was returned to action as an anti-aircraft position. It was also armed with two 5½in guns taken from HMS *Hood*. In 1941 the first of the Maunsell Forts to be placed in the Thames estuary was towed past Coalhouse Point.

The fort was also used as a site to deal with the danger from German magnetic mines. Equipment in the river checked the polarity of ships leaving the Thames on their way out to sea. The ships were treated by passing an electric current through

Coalhouse Fort gateway, which is less elaborate than its near neighbour at Tilbury.

A radar tower close to the Second World War gun emplacements.

Above: *Second World War gun emplacements on the bank of the Thames close to the fort.*

Left: *A spigot mortar emplacement. These are rare as they are usually sunk into the ground, but the two at Coalhouse Fort are both on the surface.*

them while they were in port, which lessened the chance of them being damaged by magnetic mines. Any ships found still to be magnetic by the fort were sent back to be treated again. An anti-aircraft battery was also constructed close to the fort at Bowaters Farm. These sites were at first operated by territorials.

The fort and the batteries were often bombed and machine-gunned by enemy aircraft during the conflict. There was a minefield that was controlled from a two-storey pillbox which can still be seen today. There are also two surviving examples of spigot mortar emplacements.

Although the fort was at first manned by the Royal Artillery, it was later taken over by the East Tilbury Home Guard. They must have been very experienced in using the guns as they won a competition for rapid loading at Shoebury.

The fort was disarmed again after the war for the final time and used for a short while to train cadets. It was then leased to the nearby Bata shoe company for storage until taken over by Thurrock Council in the early 1960s.

The fort was recently entered into *Restoration*, a BBC programme featuring ancient monuments. Each building competes for renovation funds provided by the BBC. Unfortunately Coalhouse Fort was not one of those chosen.

The site has, however, been improved and the fort is now surrounded by large areas of parkland and picnic areas.

COLCHESTER

During the First World War some of the well-known war poets were inspired by the Essex countryside, and in the Second World War the beautiful scenery was again an influence on a creative member of the forces. Ross Parker was based at Colchester Barracks. When he needed peace and quiet to work in, he found tranquillity in the unusual form of one of the pillboxes close to the barracks. No one is certain which pillbox he used, as there were three close to Roman Way Camp. What is certain is that he composed two of Britain's best-known wartime songs, 'We'll Meet Again' and 'There'll Always be an England', while based at Colchester.

In 1940 the Australians came to Colchester. They were led by a band playing 'Waltzing Matilda' and were a very strange sight in their cowboy-type hats. Their headquarters were in London Road, which was secretly visited by the King on 30 October.

The Australians were followed by New Zealanders, Canadians and Indians, who brought trains of packhorses. The New Zealanders were not new to Essex; they had a base in Hornchurch during the First World War. It was the Indian troops' job to negotiate areas where motor vehicles could not reach by using their packhorses. There were also Czechs, who were visited by their President at Wivenhoe Park in 1943. Dutch seamen were also based in the town and the Dutch resistance were trained at nearby Warley Barracks. Poles gave musical concerts at Manningtree.

Colchester took on a multinational atmosphere. It didn't stop shortages, however. By Christmas the only things on sale for presents were books, and the bookshops were always full of soldiers. The visitors also entered into the social life of the town, which went down well with the young women as most eligible young Englishmen were off fighting somewhere else in the world. Over 500 girls from Essex married Canadians during the war years, but this number was bettered by the number of marriages of Essex girls to the Americans who arrived later. Cherry Tree Camp in Mersea Road became a Canadian military hospital.

The foreign troops were only a supplement to the large numbers of British troops in the town. Colchester Garrison had been extended in 1938 by building numerous huts and several barrack squares. After Dunkirk it became a training centre for the new army. Thousands of recruits were trained and then passed on to other areas. The progress in the way war was fought was obvious in the way the troops in the town were affected. The use of packhorses was dropped and horses finally disappeared as a means of transport for military men. In 1939 the 5th Royal Iniskilling Dragoons had to bid farewell to their horses at the cavalry barracks. Traditional cavalry were no longer required in modern warfare.

By 1941 invasion scares became serious and the public were often ordered off the streets for invasion manoeuvres. Canadian artillery set up guns around the town and messages were flashed across the screens in cinemas recalling soldiers to their units. The atmosphere was very tense.

Rumours started that Colchester would be evacuated of civilians to make room for American soldiers, who began to arrive in the summer of 1942. By Christmas it seemed as if the Americans had taken over the town. They had opened clubs for their troops, including one just for black troops. One of the strange customs that the

The officers' mess, Hyderabad Barracks, Colchester.

The military hospital, Colchester.

Americans brought with them was segregation between black and white, which was still the norm in America at that time.

The better wages the American received, and a seemingly endless supply of items that they had which had been scarce for years in Britain, sometimes led to bad feeling between locals and the new arrivals. At times the Americans were seen as standoffish by locals who tried to be friendly. This was because the American troops had been told that the British were very short of food and that they should not accept invitations to go into their homes and eat when rationing was so severe.

The American Air Force also arrived and more than ten new aerodromes were constructed in the area and added to the British ones already in operation.

In the years leading up to the Second World War there had been a lot of violence involving soldiers and locals. The Military Police, with help from the local police force, were kept very busy. The problems were only solved when most young men from the area were themselves called up to join the army.

Military crime was also to have an effect on Colchester after the war. In 1946 there was a riot at the military prison in Aldershot which resulted in the building being so badly damaged that it was decided to close it permanently. This left Colchester as the only military prison in the country.

The postwar years were the heyday of National Service. The popular image is of innocent young men being forced into the army and being scared by the discipline meted out by harsh NCOs. No doubt this was true of many of the National

A PoW letter from Essex camp no. 186 in Colchester. Note 'Written in German' at the top of the letter and the 'Passed' by the censor stamp.

Berechurch Hall prisoner of war camp no. 186.

An Essex Yeomanry badge. The Latin motto translates as 'An Ornament and a Safeguard'. The Yeomanry became a territorial unit in 1920 and an artillery unit in 1921. They took part in numerous battles during the Second World War.

Servicemen, perhaps even the majority. There were also, however, many others who enjoyed their service time. There were constant violent incidents as the army tradition of taking in the dregs of society continued. Many of the new recruits came from prison to the army and ended up in the army version of confinement. Colchester was no different in this. Some recruits who were later to make a name as major criminals in London started their army service by attacking the first NCO to give them an order. The military prison wall was refurbished in 1987 when a new multistorey barrack block was built to the west of the prison as part of Lille Barracks.

As well as being one of the oldest towns in Britain, Colchester also has the oldest barracks and is the third largest establishment in the country with nearly 2,000 army quarters and 5,000 acres of land owned. One advantage of this for the town is that land used for manoeuvres will continue as countryside and not be built on.

The soldiers from the barracks are a common sight in the town, as are their families; many schools have a majority of army children on their roll. There are also many cases of army involvement in the community: military bands often play in schools; numerous charities have been helped by local troops; soldiers also helped clear up after the gales in 1987 and are always available if there is any other crisis.

There have recently been plans to relocate the barracks further to the south; the older buildings of the present barracks are to be developed for residential use. The £1 billion contract was not signed until 2004, two years late, due to planning problems.

Colchester is now the home of the 3rd Battalion the Parachute Regiment at Hyderabad Barracks. They are part of a new 16 Air Assault Brigade. They are the highest readiness unit in the brigade and are deployable by parachute, aircraft and helicopter.

DAGENHAM

Although Dagenham was not the site of a large army base, it is included as a good example of how industry played such a large part in the war effort in the Second World War, and of how closely involved the military were in protecting important industrial sites.

A pillbox at the rear of Western Avenue, Dagenham.

A line of anti-tank defences that run along the back of Western Avenue and alongside the District Line.

For much of the Second World War, the area east of the A130 was restricted to all unauthorised persons. Everyone had to carry an identity card and no unauthorised person was allowed within 10 miles of the coast. Anti-tank ditch defences were erected along with pillboxes in many areas, even as far inland as Dagenham, where workers just turned up one day and erected tank traps and pillboxes in fields close to the Thames.

These defences were also close to the Sterling factory, which had begun to produce machine guns at the beginning of the war. It was a weapon that the British Army was very short of. Winston Churchill had been involved in arranging for arms expert George Patchett to be removed from Czechoslovakia, where he was working, just before the Germans invaded. It had all the ingredients of a great spy story. Patchett was then installed into the Sterling Dagenham factory where he designed a machine gun to replace the Lancaster model they had been producing. The Lancaster had been based on an obsolete German weapon.

The gun went into production in the factory, which was by then mainly run by a female workforce. The women workers did such long hours that the company employed its own hairdresser. Although some bomb damage did occur at the site, it did not stop production of the machine guns, which became important weapons in the British army for a number of years during and after the war.

The May & Baker chemical works was also close to the defences that were erected in Dagenham. At the beginning of the war large quantities of the factory's products were taken away and stored in areas of the country thought to be less at risk of

Two matchbox covers from local Barking company J. John Masters from a series showing different rank markings from the forces. Another example of how business played on the war to help sales.

Below: *Ford at Dagenham was hit by several enemy bombs during the war but none of them held up production for long.* (Ford Motor Company)

Ford workers help to clear up the mess after another direct hit. (Ford Motor Company)

bombing than the Dagenham site. One of these areas was railway sidings in Wales. A number of underground shelters were built on the factory site, and the buildings were painted in camouflage colours. There were direct telephone links with nearby RAF Hornchurch and anti-aircraft sites in Dagenham and Barking in case of any attack.

In 1940 a Home Guard unit was formed to protect the May & Baker factory. In an exercise paratroopers based at Hornchurch airbase attacked the factory; while the Home Guard were protecting the back of the factory, the works fire brigade drove the parachutists off at the front of the works using their hoses.

The works fire brigade had a hand in more serious matters when a bomb set fire to a large amount of inflammable material that was dangerous when sprayed with water. Two of the works firemen, W. Beeson and L. Fisher, were awarded the George Medal for using cement powder to put out the fire. There is a story that when the local fire brigade arrived to help, they tried to use water despite warnings. One of the medal winners, Fisher, supposedly knocked out the fire chief with one punch and took charge of the situation himself.

As with their neighbours Sterling, a large number of their workers during the war were women. However, they were not allowed to do night work. An unusual addition to the May & Baker workforce was around fifty Italian prisoners of war, who were housed in a YMCA building close to the main entrance to the factory.

HARWICH

What happened during the war years in Harwich and the areas around it was one of the most closely guarded secrets of the war, as was the number of ships and smaller boats lost to enemy action. One of the hardest hit local companies was Everards coal boats, which served gasworks in Essex. They lost nineteen boats during the war years.

The LNER fleet that had sailed from Harwich also suffered many losses. Harwich was closed as a passenger port at the beginning of the war, but the fleet was still in use. Five of its thirteen vessels were lost at sea and many others were damaged, including train ferries. The worst disaster was the sinking of the *Amsterdam* which had been converted to a hospital ship. It hit a mine off the French coast in 1944 and

Harwich redoubt was left to decay after some postwar use, but has now been renovated and is open to the public.

The central area of the redoubt, showing the rooms built into the walls.

sank. The heavy loss of life included many members of the crew who were from Harwich and Dovercourt.

In the Second World War the strongest defences were placed on the Felixstowe side of the harbour, as had happened in the past. New forts and batteries were added as well as improvements to Landguard Fort.

There were also improvements to defences on the Essex side of the river. Concrete gun placements were added to Beacon Hill to protect the guns along with anti-aircraft weapons. Underground magazines were dug to store ammunition, which was fed to the guns using mechanical hoists. Large observation towers were also added. This changed the appearance of the fort, which until then had not been very noticeable from the sea.

Also added to the site during the war were concrete anti-aircraft covers for the larger guns. One of these had a Bofors anti-aircraft gun on top of it, and there were also three Lewis guns. Searchlights were placed around the perimeter of the fort. The guns were manned by territorials raised from the local area, who were usually men too young to serve abroad. As they got older they were often transferred to other units. The gun crews were from units of the Royal Artillery and Royal Engineers.

Ships of the Royal Naval Reserve Fleet in Harwich harbour during the Second World War.

The Second World War defences at Beacon Hill have not been as lucky as the redoubt. The gun placements are crumbling and covered in graffiti.

The observation tower on Beacon Hill is now too dangerous to climb.

The radar tower from the Second World War at Beacon Hill is now fenced off to keep the public out tand has survived slightly better than other Beacon Hill buildings.

It was the Suffolk Heavy Regiment Royal Artillery who manned the guns and the Fortress Company Royal Engineers who manned the searchlights. The personnel often changed with men being transferred to other units and mainly sent abroad.

Harwich was also the base of a naval force of two flotillas of cruisers and destroyers during the Second World War. At the beginning of the war it was suspected that the Germans were dropping some new type of weapon. On one occasion German planes were allowed to fly over without being fired upon by anti-aircraft guns and to drop their bombs and other items while being observed. Three destroyers were then sent out to retrieve what the planes had dropped. Unfortunately they were magnetic mines. One of the ships, HMS *Gypsy*, found a mine, which stuck to the ship's side and sunk it, resulting in numerous casualties. Harwich along with much of the Thames Estuary suffered from numerous raids during the so-called Phoney War, which mainly involved the dropping of magnetic mines into the coastal waters and rivers.

The naval headquarters in Harwich during the Second World War were based in the Great Eastern Hotel. The Napoleonic redoubt was also used during the war, and at one time was a detention centre for British soldiers.

After the war the redoubt was taken over by Civil Defence and used for nuclear exercises. Once they finished with it, the redoubt was left to deteriorate like the other defences in the town. The redoubt has since been restored, but the Second World War defences at Beacon Hill are now in a very sorry state of repair.

HORNCHURCH

During the 1930s Hornchurch aerodrome was fully operational and held a number of air shows that attracted thousands of visitors. What seems strange now was that among the VIP guests were high-ranking members of the Luftwaffe.

The relaxed attitude of the 1930s ended as the decade drew to a close. Fighter planes from Hornchurch were the first to be involved in action in the Second World War in the skies over Essex. Unfortunately, what became known as the Battle of Barking Creek did not involve any enemy aircraft. Reports came in of an unidentified aircraft approaching across the North Sea. It was in fact a British Blenheim bomber, but Hurricanes were sent out from North Weald and Spitfires from Hornchurch to intercept it. Two of the Hurricanes were then mistakenly shot down by the Spitfires. The plane that started the panic was also shot down by anti-aircraft fire. The beginning of the war was not very successful for the RAF. Thankfully for Britain it got much better.

This early disaster did not deter a film company from using Hornchurch as the location for a film about the RAF called *The Lion Has Wings*. The film showed that many of the men at the base were living in tents and although they flew a lot, they had very few encounters with the enemy during the early months of the war.

When the Battle of Britain started pilots from Hornchurch were as involved in fighting the Luftwaffe as those from any other airfield, as Hornchurch was often on

The entrance to what was one of the air raid shelters at Hornchurch Airfield. Now part of the car park at the country park that covers much of the site.

the route of the German planes as they made their way towards London. In the early part of the war pilots from Hornchurch were responsible for protecting convoys in the Channel.

Representatives of the East India Company presented eight Spitfires to no. 65 Squadron at the airfield and a cheque for £55,000 towards payment for more. The planes became part of the East India Squadron. It was a welcome return to the county by the company that had once owned the barracks at Warley, which had been used by the company army.

The pilots at Hornchurch destroyed a large number of enemy aircraft during the course of the war, but unfortunately many of the pilots died while doing their duty and defending Britain. Those on the ground on the airfields suffered from numerous attacks; there were over twenty, and they did not stop until almost the end of the war. In 1945 a V2 rocket landed on the aerodrome, destroying many of the buildings, including the NAAFI. There were other near misses when rockets fell on the surrounding area, resulting in civilian casualties.

Hornchurch also had a dummy airfield at Bulphan. As with other dummy sites, there were wooden aircraft that were supposed to fool the enemy. They were sometimes moved around by airmen to make the site seem more realistic.

The airfield did not close at the end of the war as it had done in the First World War. As well as carrying out the duties of the peacetime RAF, there were several well-attended air shows during the 1950s, often attracting over 20,000 visitors. The end came 1962, when it was finally closed and put up for auction.

Part of the land was used for building, and the resulting streets of houses brought back memories of the past. A famous name arrived at Hornchurch in 1939: John Mungo Park, a descendant of the explorer of Africa, Alexander Mungo Park. Part of the locality inherited the name Mungo Park, so it became well known. The memory of the airfield is also preserved in the Airfield estate, which is built on part of it. The roads on the estate are named after the pilots who served and often died at Hornchurch.

After going through a number of uses, including gravel extraction and as a landfill site for rubbish, the rest of the site is now a country park with some remaining mementoes of the airfield, such as the defensive gun emplacements and pillboxes. There is also an underground shelter, the entrance to which now stands in the car park.

One of the three pillboxes that have survived the various uses that Hornchurch Airfield has been through since its closure.

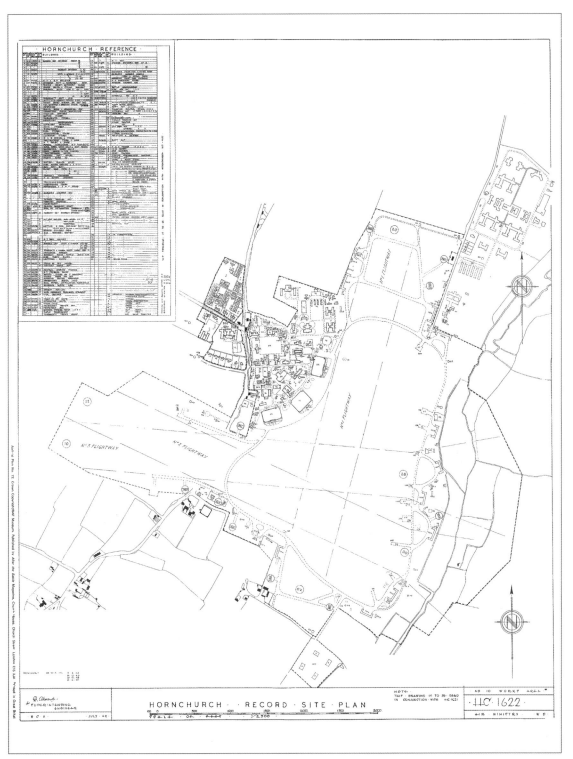

A plan of Hornchurch Airfield in 1942.

KELVEDON HATCH

The Cold War that quickly followed the end of the Second World War led to another round of military building in Essex. This was a time when the world became increasingly worried about the disastrous outcome of possible nuclear conflict, especially after seeing the results of the nuclear attacks on Japan. Although the two main protagonists in the Cold War were the USSR and the USA, Britain, and hence Essex, was in the front line when it came to danger from the Soviet nuclear missiles.

As a result of the threat, the government built a series of secret deep bunkers, to protect them from nuclear explosions. The country would be run from these bunkers by what was left of the government and the military in the event of a nuclear attack. They also built several smaller bunkers throughout the county which were used as bases for the Royal Observer Corps.

One of the larger bunkers was built in rural Essex in Kelvedon Hatch in 1953. It is hidden underneath a bungalow and reaches 75ft underground. The walls are 10ft

The bungalow that hides the entrance to the bunker. (Kelvedon Hatch Secret Bunker)

Some civil defence equipment. The blackboard lists the effects on the public of a nuclear attack. (Kelvedon Hatch Secret Bunker)

thick. Hard as it is to believe, the locals were apparently unaware of what was built beneath them.

The original plan was that the bunker would be an operations centre for RAF Fighter Command in the Metropolitan Sector. It later became the UK's Warning and Monitoring Metropolitan Sector HQ. It then changed to a more civil-based use, becoming the regional Home Office Bunker for London and finally Regional Government Headquarters.

The bunker is big enough to hold up to 600 people, possibly including the prime minister. The building had its own water supply, electricity generators, radar, BBC studio and a room where nuclear experts could discover where the fallout would be most lethal above them.

Possible use of the bunker became less likely as the Cold War came to an end. In 1993 the bunker was sold by the government to the farmer who owned the land it was built underneath. It has now been opened to the public as a Cold War Museum.

MALDON

Although the barracks of the Napoleonic era were not rebuilt in Maldon during the Second World War, the town did, along with most of Essex, suffer from action from the skies. In one large raid in August 1940 nearly 100 enemy aircraft, including thirty-six Heinkel bombers, attacked airfields in Hornchurch and North Weald. Fierce opposition by the RAF greeted them and several of the Germans were shot down and crashed all over Essex: in many cases the crews were taken prisoner.

One of the Heinkels was shot down between Maldon and Heybridge. The result must have been repeated in numerous parts of the county at various times during the war. One of the crew parachuted to safety and was pursued and captured as he drifted to the ground by local man Fred Yuill, on a bicycle. Yuill was a serving Royal Marine home on leave. He found the German injured and stayed with him until the Air Raid Police arrived.

PURFLEET

In 1941 the Purfleet base was used in exercises based on the supposition that an enemy battalion had landed from the river at Purfleet and was on its way to attack Hornchurch aerodrome. The enemy were met by troops defending the airfield. There were other manoeuvres between Purfleet and Hornchurch. The Purfleet rifle

The last remaining magazine building at Purfleet. It is now a military museum.

The clock tower that marked the entrance to the magazine and barracks.

ranges were also used for bombing practice by Spitfires and for training purposes by both regular army and Home Guard units.

A section of the Territorial Army, Royal Artillery, were based at Beacon Hill near the Purfleet Camp. The Lewis gun they had was supposed to be a defence against enemy aircraft, but was not very useful in that capacity. There were also more powerful anti-aircraft defences at Purfleet with one 3in gun and twenty lighter weapons.

No doubt many of the men from Purfleet went off to fight in the war, but some gave their lives without leaving the camp. Two sergeants of the Middlesex Regiment were killed when they were in a hut that exploded. It is thought that they were examining a mortar at the time. Another mortar accident led to nine men from the Home Guard being injured, one fatally. They were using a spigot mortar on the rifle ranges at the time of the accident.

The largest influx of troops into the Purfleet area was during preparations for D-Day. The Purfleet rifle ranges were used as a gathering area, being close to the Thames where the men could board waiting ships. Purfleet and other barracks all

The training ship Cornwall *that was moored off Purfleet.*

over the county were bursting at the seams with men waiting to embark for the beaches of Normandy. The Stevedore Company Royal Engineers were at Purfleet in 1944, as were the Orset 26th Port Detachment RASC. There were also large tented camps at nearby Belhus Park and at Orset Golf Course.

Another camp had already been set up at Purfleet in 1943. This was camp 286, a prisoner of war camp for Italians who were used to work on local farms. German prisoners began to be brought back from France soon after D-Day and were also taken to Purfleet. Camps 654 and 655 were mainly tented camps with a few more permanent buildings for German PoWs.

Purfleet base had a football team that played against other units in the area, including Hornchurch aerodrome. There is no doubt that some fine footballers were in the forces and graced several of these games. There was also for some time a naval training ship, the *Cornwall*, moored in the river.

A decline seems to have set in at the magazine after the war, as it was by then being used as a barracks for national servicemen. Purfleet came in for some heavy criticism in 1953, as did its commanding officer, Lieutenant Colonel Edward Trustler, who had been brought back from Hong Kong to clean up the base. At this time it was a Royal Engineers' embarkation camp and thieving and scrounging were said to be rife, which again seems to disprove the idea of well-behaved, cowed national service recruits.

An incident involving the new commanding officer was reported in several daily national newspapers. The Lieutenant-Colonel was court-martialled for allegedly caning an 18-year-old gunner. The gunner had been absent without leave and had stolen some women's clothing.

The commanding officer was described as a strong disciplinarian, and he admitted caning the gunner twice. He was severely reprimanded and lost two years' seniority. During the court-martial the conditions at Purfleet barracks were described as appalling. Perhaps this was one of the reasons for the demise of the site not long afterwards.

The rifle ranges at Purfleet actually reached up to Rainham, and were still visible from Ferry Lane, Rainham, in the 1970s. New roads and industry seemed to have led to their removal along with other local military sites

The only remaining part of the Purfleet base is one of the original magazine buildings. It is situated between the Royal Hotel and a modern housing estate that covers the site of the rest of the magazine and now houses the Purfleet Heritage Centre, which is a museum of local military history, including a large collection of memorabilia from Hornchurch Aerodrome.

SHOEBURYNESS

One of the problems with researching Essex during the Second World War is that censorship prevented much of what happened from being reported. This was nowhere more evident than when Shoeburyness Barracks was opened to the national press in 1939. It was obvious to any reader of the articles where the reports were

The badge of the Experimental Establishment, Shoeburyness.

from because Shoeburyness was the only experimental gunnery site in the country, but the reporters were still not allowed to name the site.

The outbreak of war led to a sharp increase in the number of men in the barracks, who were mainly Gunner reservists. The regiments based there were being brought up to strength before being sent to France. The camp also welcomed hundreds of militiamen who came to be trained there. The recruits were based in the old ranges until the end of the war.

Extra accommodation had to be found for the men who moved through the camp throughout the war. Many of them were put up in wooden huts erected on the sports field.

Several batteries of guns were deployed within the ranges at Shoeburyness after the retreat from Dunkirk. So much equipment had been lost however that most of the guns were leftovers from the First World War.

As added protection, part of the beach was mined and barbed wire was stretched along the dangerous area as added defence from an attack from the river and to keep out anyone from the landward side. Unfortunately, in the tradition of young people in the area who had been injured in the past, a young boy crawled under the wire and set off a mine, losing his leg. A soldier who went to his aid also set off a mine and was killed.

Another added defence were the sea forts erected in the Thames Estuary, named Maunsell Forts after their designer, architect Guy Maunsell. There were four and their remains can still be seen. A boom was also stretched across the river from both

The gateway to what was Shoeburyness Barracks. It is now an exclusive housing estate with both original and new buildings for sale as homes.

A notice board on the outside of the wall of Shoeburyness Barracks. Although the barracks are now closed, the board still carries copies of military bye-laws.

banks to reduce the size of the entrance to the river for shipping. The open area in the centre could also be closed, using a submarine net.

Many of the men who became famous in television and radio after the war were making their mark in wartime military entertainment, and among them was Shoeburyness's Gunner Frankie Howerd, who was a star of the concerts in the Garrison Theatre in the early years of the war.

The gunnery school was in danger of air attacks because of its proximity to the ships gathered in the Thames. This led to it being moved away from Shoeburyness. The move began the gradual decline of the site from which it never really recovered.

The area around Southend was one of the reception areas for evacuated children early in the war, but it was later necessary to evacuate them elsewhere, and there was pressure on adults to leave as well. The sense of this move was seen in 1940 when fifty Heinkels dropped their cargo of bombs over Shoeburyness. Surprisingly, fatalities were very few.

Winston Churchill visited the site on a number of occasions, the first time in 1941 to watch a rocket demonstration. During the visit he supposedly spilt a glass of wine down his trousers.

There were celebrations throughout the country at the end of the war and at Shoeburyness the garrison held a victory show. It was a way of thanking the locals for their support. Many of the weapons on display at the show had until then been top secret.

The biggest change to Shoeburyness came after the war. The concentration on weapons that fired on shipping was replaced by the testing of bombs that could be dropped from planes. Along with this was its use for the storage of numerous old planes; some were used for weapon testing while others were scrapped, including a large number of Spitfires.

The end for the base came in 1998 when the ranges were closed. It is now possible to buy a home in what was once the barracks. A maisonette was on offer in 2004 for just under £200,000. It was described as being within the historic garrison with views towards the chapel. Since the closure of the garrison, the chapel, St Paul's, has been stripped of its military memorials, which have been moved to either Colchester or Woolwich.

The wall of the barracks is still in place, and inside there is an assortment of new houses and original buildings of the old barracks now converted for residential use. There is still a signpost on the wall outside bearing notices of military bye-laws relating to the firing ranges.

Although Foulness was acquired during the First World War, it was not until after the Second World War that full use was made of it. It was also used in the development of nuclear weapons during the Cold War.

Control of Foulness by the government has led to it becoming cut off from the rest of Essex. It is very difficult to visit the island; even the local MP, Teddy Taylor, had trouble obtaining a pass to cross the bridge to the island. There is now a civilian population of about 200, mainly involved in farming. There is also still an explosives testing station on Foulness, which is owned by the Ministry of Defence but run by an agency called Qineti Q.

Despite the tight security on the island, there is still a connection with the past of the Shoeburyness site. Although a pass is needed to cross the bridge, an old bye-law allows boats to land to collect water from the George and Dragon pub, the only one on the island. In the 1800s boats full of sightseers used to come ashore and watch the experiments at Shoeburyness.

SOUTHEND

The pier at Southend played a big part in the war effort during the Second World War. Ships were moored at the end of the structure and the pier railway was in constant use carrying servicemen to their ships and wounded back to the shore. Part of the train was adapted to carry stretchers.

The ships that entered the Thames during the war years were monitored by the men on the pier who controlled the naval gateway to London. The Navy took over the pier in 1939 and it was closed to the public. Enemy planes attacked it on several occasions, machine-gunning it and dropping magnetic mines round it.

Preparations for a war were under way and camps for soldiers were already established, such as Hawkwell Camp near Southend in 1937. Here are officers and men of the 1st Anti-Aircraft Division Royal Army Service Corps (TA), Supply Section.

Officers of an unidentified RASC unit.

Southend Pier became the base for the naval authorities that controlled shipping in the Thames during the war. The two paddle steamers shown at the pier in this pre-war photograph both went to Dunkirk. The Crested Eagle *was bombed and sank with the loss of 300 lives. The* Royal Eagle *made three trips to Dunkirk and later became an anti-aircraft boat on the Thames.*

The biggest event in the river off the pier was when the Thames filled with ships in preparation for D-Day. Most of the ships were destined for the beaches of Normandy, but some never made the trip, including the American ship *Richard Montgomery* which sank off Thorpe Bay full of ammunition and explosives, much of which is still there today.

It must have been strange for the locals when they woke on the morning of D-Day to find the river empty of shipping, which had all sailed during the night. Many of the ships soon returned, however, bringing back the wounded and taking more reinforcements across to the beaches of Normandy for the push into France.

TILBURY FORT

The fort was garrisoned until the 1920s but then fell into disuse until the war. During the Second World War the Home Guard manned it. At first the gun operations room which controlled the anti-aircraft guns on the Thames and the Medway was based in the chapel in the fort, but it was then moved to a specially built building in Vange in 1940. Part of the old soldiers' barracks building was destroyed by bombing during the war and later demolished. The officers' barracks are still standing.

The Tilbury Fort gateway in the 1930s.

The Tilbury gateway today. It has remained unchanged over the centuries.

The officers' barracks inside Tilbury Fort. The chimneys of the power station are visible in the background. The men's barracks were bombed in the war and were then demolished.

The inside of the gateway and chapel of Tilbury Fort.

In 1942 the naval training ship *Exmouth* was towed from its normal position further upriver at Grays to Tilbury for repairs. The waste ground around the fort was used to detonate unexploded bombs that were often brought from other areas. In the build-up to D-Day the whole of Tilbury became a storage area for military vehicles and there was a tented army camp inside the docks.

The men based at the fort had a football team that played other military units in the area. Many buildings have been added during the life of the fort, and others demolished. In 1980 the fort became a national monument. It has been used in television programmes such as the *Sharpe* series based on the Napoleonic War.

The fort is still very isolated with only the World's End public house close to it, and it is easy to imagine how remote it would have seemed before the docks and power station were built close by.

WARLEY

During the war Warley, along with other Essex barracks, was used to train new recruits. Members of the Dutch resistance also spent time training at the barracks.

The 2nd Battalion the Essex Regiment was based at Warley until they went to France on 1 September 1939. They were not there long, however, as they were part of the army that was evacuated from the beaches of Dunkirk the following May.

During the early 1950s Warley was used as a training depot for the Essex Regiment for national service recruits. They spent six weeks drilling and polishing at

Inside the Essex Regiment Chapel at Warley.

The Essex Regiment Chapel today. The bell tower was added in the 1950s as a war memorial.

Warley before moving on to other postings. They would march from the barracks to Brentwood station and board a train on the first leg of their journey. Many of them were posted to Germany, where they found barracks that were far superior to those at Warley, which were by then quite dated. The National Servicemen would later return to the camp from their postings to be demobbed.

By the 1950s Warley had partly reverted to its origins as a camp under canvas. A number of soldiers slept in tents pitched on the sports field. Further building work was carried out to the Garrison Church in 1955 when a bell tower was added as a war memorial.

In 1956 a battalion of National Servicemen who had come to Warley to be demobbed arrived at Brentwood station and were cheered by the customers at local pubs as they marched to the barracks. They found the barracks to be a collection of ancient buildings, some of which were wooden structures. Much of the cooking was still being done on wood-burning stoves.

In 1958 the Essex Regiment became part of the Anglian Regiment and Warley was empty for some time. Most of the buildings were demolished after the closure of the barracks in 1960, but one of the wooden buildings, the Garrison Engineers' office, went on to have a new lease of life when it was sold to Ongar Scout Group.

A plaque in the wall of the chapel.

The rear of Keyes Community Hall in Eagle Way. The building was the gymnasium of Warley Barracks. The back of the building is the only original face; the other sides of the building all have modern extensions.

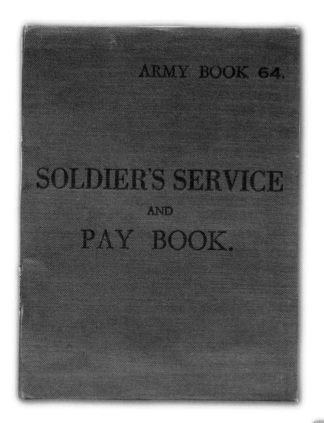

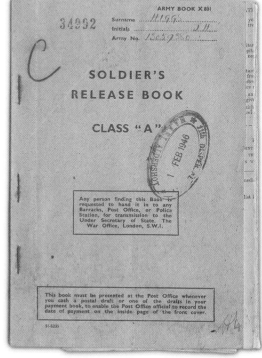

A soldier's service and pay book and a release book for J.H. Higgs, a member of the Essex Regiment in the Second World War.

They took the building down and rebuilt it in Ongar in 1962. The only remaining buildings are the chapel, officers' mess and the old gymnasium, which is now a local community hall.

The museum collection of the Essex Regiment was moved to Chelmsford. Although hardly any of the buildings survive there are still some reminders in the locality such as Eagle Way, a road named after the taking of a French Eagle (a standard) by one of the Essex Regiment's predecessors during the Napoleonic Wars.

So many of the local population worked and had involvement with the barracks throughout its history that it became an important part of the local community. Its demise had an effect that was felt far beyond its military residents.

WEELEY

By the time the Home Guard had been established, Winston Churchill's plans for home defence had gone much further than the idea of squads of elderly men volunteering to protect their local areas. He wanted to create the Auxiliary Force, that is, small groups of highly trained, well-armed men who would go to ground in the event of an invasion. They would then carry out acts of sabotage in the enemy's rear, such as destroying railway lines and bridges. They would be similar to the SOE, which was conducting such operations in occupied Europe. The existence of these units was a well-kept secret during the war, and it was only many years later that knowledge of them became public.

One of these units was based in Weeley. All the groups were located close to the coast so that they could operate behind enemy lines. There were six men in the group. They had an underground bunker in the grounds of Weeley Hall Wood, and even their families did not know the task they had been set. They were very well armed and their job was to harry the enemy in the event of an invasion. During one invasion scare in Harwich, the Weeley group spent two days in their hideout, waiting to attack the enemy. If the Germans had invaded and these men had been caught, they may not have been treated as prisoners of war, but have been shot. Fortunately, they never had to find out which it would be.

Bibliography

BOOKS AND NEWSPAPERS

Addison, W., *Essex Heyday*, Dent, 1949

Barking, East Ham & Ilford Advertiser, August 1914, December 1914, October 1915, August 1916

Benham, H., *Essex at War*, Essex County Standard, 1945

Benton, T., *The Changing Face of Hornchurch*, Sutton, 2001

Bingley, R., Daniel Defoe, 'His Trail Uncovered', *Panorama 27*, Journal of Thurrock Local History Society

Brandon, D., *Stand and Deliver*, Sutton, 2001

Brown, A., *Essex at Work*, Essex County Council, 1969

——, *Chartism in Essex and Suffolk*, Essex Record Office, 1982

Brown, D., *Weeley through the Ages*, Parochial Church Council, 1996

Burrows, J., 'Tilbury Fort', *Journal of British Archaeological Association*, 1932

Callahan, R., *The East India Company and Army Reform*, Harvard University, 1972

Carter, M., ' The Fort of Othona and the Chapel of St Peter on the Wall, Bradwell', Provost and Chapter of Chelmsford, 1967

Carter, T., *Historical Record of the 44th or East Essex Regiment*, Gale & Poulden, 1887

Chelmsford Chronicle, July 1794, October 1794, May 1795, December 1801, March 1802, 30 July 1808, April 1856

Colchester Gazette, 25 May 1816

Colchester Guide, Jarrold Publishing

Colchester 800: 1189–1989, Colchester Arts Association

Cooke, W. (ed.), *Edward Thomas*, Everyman, 1997

Crocker, G., *The Gunpowder Industry*, Shire Publications, 1986

Cruickshank, D., *Invasion*, Boxtree, 2001

Daily Mirror, 9 January 1953

'Dagenham Childhood', Students of Eastbrook School, Dagenham, 1997

David, S., *Homicidal Earl*, Little, Brown, 1997

Edwards, A., *History of Essex*, Phillimore, 2000

Essex Chronicle, 22 April 1884

Essex Police Notebook, issue 23

Essex Review, 'Martello Towers', vol. 40; 'Record of Mark Crummie', vol. 55

Evans, B., *Bygone Barking*, Phillimore, 1991

——, *Hornchurch and Upminster*, Phillimore, 1990

——, *Romford, Collier Row and Gidea Park*, Phillimore, 1994

——, *Romford Heritage*, Sutton, 2002

Evening Journal, 30 November 1915

Filby, J. and Clark, G., *Not All Airmen Fly*, Epping Forest District Council, 1994

Forbes, A., *Barracks, Bivouacs and Battles*, Macmillan, 1897

Frogley, 'Mr Frogley's Barking, 1st Selection, Barking and Dagenham', 2002

——, 'Mr Frogley's Barking, 2nd Selection, Barking and Dagenham', 2003

Gifford, P., *Resist the Invader*, Essex Libraries, 1982

Great War 1914–18, Essex Telegraph Ltd, 1923

Greenwood, P., 'Uphall Camp, An Iron Age Fortification', *London Archaeologist*, Autumn 1989

Grieve, H., 'The Sleepers and the Shadows', Essex Record Office, 1994

Harper, G., *Warley Magna to Great Warley*, Dickens, 1956

Herbert, A., *The War Story of Southend Pier*, Southend on Sea, 1945

Hill, T., *Guns and Gunners*, Baron, 1999

History of Havering, souvenir booklet, Havering (nd)

Hope, Montcrieff A., *Essex*, A. & C. Black

Jarvis, S., *Essex: A County History*, Countryside Books, 1993

Lewis, G., *Behind the Walls*, Ian Henry, 1996

Leyin, A., 'Purfleet Gunpowder Magazine', *Panorama 41*, Journal of the Thurrock Local History Society

Marriage, J., *Maldon and the Blackwater Estuary*, Phillimore, 1996

Martin, G., *The Story of Colchester*, Bentham, 1959

May, T., *Military Barracks*, Shire Books, 2002

Mee, A., *Essex*, Hodder & Stoughton, 1942

Morgan, G., *Forgotten Thameside*, Thames Books, 1951

Nunn, P. and Wyatt, A., *Heinkels over Heybridge*, Nunn & Wyatt, 1987

Orford, M., *The Shoebury Story*, Ian Henry, 2000

Penfold, J., *Essex County Hospital*, Penfold, Colchester, 1988

Perfect, C., *Hornchurch During the Great War*, Benham, 1920

Powell, W., 'Medieval Hospitals at East and West Tilbury and Henry VIII's Blockhouses', *Essex Archaeology & History 19*, 1988

Protection of Your House against Air Raids, Home Office, 1938

Reflector, 'Gordon, a Hero Remembered', *Panorama 27*, Journal of the Thurrock Local History Society

Roach, J., '39th Regiment of Foot and the East India Company', *Bulletin of John Rylands Library*, 41 (1958), 1–9

Royal Military Police Association website

Saunders, A., 'Tilbury Fort and Development of Artillery Fortifications in the Thames Estuary', *Antiquaries Journal*, London 40 (1960)

——, *Tilbury Fort*, HMSO, 1960

Sherry, P., *A Portrait of Victorian Colchester*, Egon, 1982
Smith, K., *Essex under Arms*, Ian Henry, 1998
Smith, R., *Hornchurch Scramble*, Grub St, 2000
Sparks, J., *The Life of Ben Franklin*
Strugnell, K., *Seagates, to the Saxon Shore*, Terence Dalton, 1973
Terry, G., *Memories of Old Romford*, 1880
Thomas, H., *Under Storm's Wing*, Carcanet, 1997
Thomas, O., *Childhood Memories of Hornchurch*, Havering, 1991
Tompkins, H., *Companions into Essex*, Methuen, 1938
Torry, G., 'Chelmsford through the Ages', *East Anglian Magazine*, 1977
Victoria History of Essex, vol. 7 (1978)
Weaver, L., *Harwich, Gateway to the Continent*, Terence Dalton, 1998
Wild, A., *East India Company*, HarperCollins, 1999
Wood, T., 'Purfleet Gunpowder Magazine', *Panorama 28*, Journal of the Thurrock
    Local History Society
Yearsley, I., *Essex Events*, Phillimore, 1999
——, *A History of Southend*, Phillimore, 2001

ESSEX RECORD OFFICE DOCUMENTS

Circular from Archbishop of Canterbury, D/P 200/1/33
Crime Report, Barrack Dept D/DEL L/4
Defence of Essex Report, T/A 218/1
Invoice, D/D CM/C1/13
Invoice, D/DCr A29
Jack Watts, T/A 235/1
Letters Concerning Threat of Invasion, D/DU 1487/2
Letters from Churchwardens and War Office, D/P 157/611
Letters to the Poor Law Commission, D/P 66/19/2
Mildmay Letters, D/Dmy/15M50/84/1
Military Memoir, T/A 218/1
Poster Naval Bounty, D/P 200 18/2
Purfleet Cuttings, T/P 110/50
Report on Purfleet, T/A 235/1
Report on Sick and Wounded, T/P 83/3
Use of Troops to Suppress Civil Disorder, D/Dby 0/2
Volunteer Pledge, D/DGg L/U
William Robinson Notebook, D/DU F129

Index